Experimental Cocktail Club

Experimental Cocktail Club

Olivier Bon, Pierre-Charles Cros, Romée de Goriainoff, Xavier Padovani

London • Paris • New York • Ibiza

MITCHELL BEAZLEY

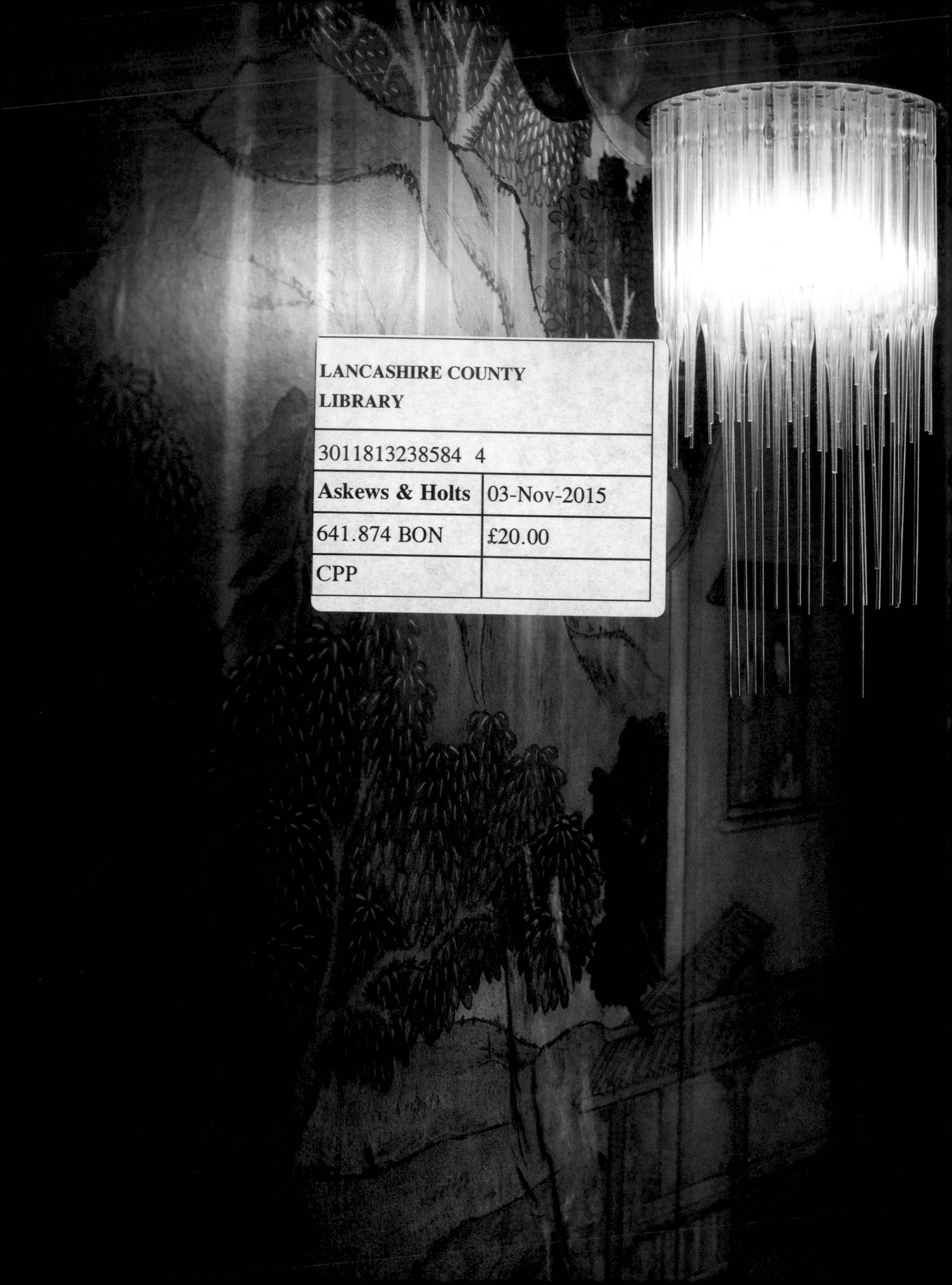

CONTENTS

Growing up in France, we had been taught from a young age to have a burning passion for good food and great drinks.

FOREWORD

In 2005, we were fresh out of university with our sights set high on doing something that wouldn't keep us stuck behind a desk for the rest of our lives. The three of us – that's Romée de Goriainoff, Pierre-Charles Cros and Olivier Bon – grew up within walking distance of each other and spent much of our youth together. That bond stuck through university and still, to this day, les Trois Garçons, as we've been called, are lifelong friends and business partners. In 2010, just before we opened our first bar outside Paris, we added our fourth partner, Xavier Padovani, to the fold and he's been with us ever since.

Since we first threw open our doors in 2007, blissfully naïve about the impending cocktail revolution on the Parisian horizon, we've had our highs and lows, but along the way we've imbibed some of the best cocktails in the world and worked alongside some of the most influential barmen and women. We've witnessed the changing landscape of the bar industry and surfed the new wave of cocktail bars that has influenced European and American cocktail culture.

We had our eyes set on expansion from day one, but it's hard to say whether or not we thought we would ever be where we are now. Our journey so far has led us to do some great things, making inevitable mistakes along the way. We've forged lifelong friendships, spent more time in aeroplanes and hotels than most, and have only just begun to understand the trials and tribulations of running businesses in multiple countries.

It goes without saying that opening a cocktail bar, and running a successful business, is not for the faint of heart. But come hell or high water – or in our case power outages, busted air conditioning and tricky plumbing – the most important thing for us is to serve up our vision of the *joyeux bordel* every night in London, Paris, Ibiza and New York.

Experimental Cocktail Club

The Original

Once upon a time, when America was suddenly devoid of cocktail bars, many barmen fled to greener pastures and set up shop in Europe. Paris's cocktail culture flourished and, in the Roaring Twenties, a golden era was born. Over time, however, cocktails fell from grace and by the Seventies, finding a decent cocktail in Paris proved to be a treasure hunt with poor results.

When we hatched the idea to open our first cocktail bar, Paris was a risk at best. No one knew one gin from the next, vodka was king, and tinctures, bitters and infusions were only whispers we heard from the far-off land of America. France had given the world stunning wines and glorious food, but cocktails remained an expensive afterthought reserved for portly men surveying the land of the hotel bar.

In 2007, Experimental Cocktail Club opened its doors on Rue Saint-Sauveur, hailing the rebirth of the French cocktail. People naturally thought we were a trio of foolish friends, but we knew we were on the brink of something good and our passion prevailed.

What we set out to do was different. Armed with the drive of youthful determination, we convinced our families and friends to support us. We would open the world's best cocktail bar in a place where no one would expect it: Paris. This isn't a story of big investors with deep pockets. It's a tale of three friends taking a blind leap into the ruthless world of bars and hoping that the landing was a safe one.

When we opened, the plan was to recreate a New York speakeasy, and to do it well. We knew we had just one chance with our money, with the bank, with our families and friends. So we planned to make the best cocktail bar in the world. Finding a space was nearly impossible. After an entire year of looking, a call came offering a place we had seen previously at a price we could afford.

Although most people would have given up during that first year, we spent our time searching, learning and being inspired. Some days were better than others, but the unwavering bond between us kept us chipping away, making our dream a reality. We went to New York to see Martin Doudoroff, who taught us to make drinks the proper way – with a jigger, something that was unheard of at the time in France. Martin gave us guidance as we developed our first cocktail menu. Not long after our trip to New York, we travelled to Lyon to see Fernando Castillon, another source of inspiration for our menu.

When we phoned New York-based designer Cuoco Black, hoping he might have a suggestion for the design of our bar, he packed his bags and flew to France. He created the interior of the space, paying homage to the brick wall and beamed structure as it still stands today. Bar tops were cut by our own hands, and mirrors were found in our grannies' attics in the French countryside. Finally, the first Experimental Cocktail Club opened on a warm night in June 2007.

From the beginning, we knew that every element in our bars held equal importance. A bar doesn't begin and end with the cocktails. This may seem obvious, and it is blatantly clear when one sits in a bar and something isn't right. Yet many bar owners who can make a smashing drink often forget it. The music, the lighting, the design and every detail in between are only pieces of the larger

puzzle. Our philosophy was the same then as it is now. Every night, in each of our bars, we strive to deliver the best drinks we can possibly make, using the freshest ingredients, with service, music and atmosphere to match the quality of the cocktails in the glasses.

People often ask about the name Experimental Cocktail Club. When we opened, the industry was in the heyday of molecular cocktails, riding on the coat-tails of molecular dining. Frankly, we are anything but. We always knew 'Cocktail Club' would be part of our name, harking back to the true post-Prohibition cocktail clubs. We fell upon the name 'Experimental' thanks to a suggestion from one of our sisters. The name was chosen to represent the overall experience in our bars: the combination of the atmosphere, the music, the clientele and the drinks into one grand experiment which we continue to polish and perfect.

When Experimental Cocktail Club first opened, many of the spirits sitting behind the bar were uncommon at the time in Paris – tequila, rye, gin and vintage spirits – so every night was a masterclass for anyone who ventured through our doors. Guests would arrive and not recognize one thing on the menu. We never wanted to be pretentious, but rather we wanted people to take the journey – the experimentation – along with us. So we would simply ask guests to try and if they didn't like it, the drink would go in the sink. It seemed to work and, months later, we were selling record amounts of tequila and Parisians were loving gin cocktails.

A few of the cocktails in this chapter are from our original menu and were our own invention. Looking back at those menus, we can see how much cocktail culture has changed since we opened, but a few of the originals still remain our signature cocktails to this day.

This was one of the first cocktails we had on our list and it still makes an appearance on the menu from time to time. It's a cool, refreshing drink that has stood the test of time. Many of our other bars have used this cocktail as inspiration to create their own variations. The Experience series is often given a new lease of life using different base spirits – gin or pisco, for example – in our bars around the world.

Experience No. 1

2 basil leaves
1 lemongrass stem, torn into pieces
50ml (2fl oz) Fair vodka
20ml (¾fl oz) fresh lemon juice
20ml (¾fl oz) elderflower cordial
ice

◆◆◆◆◆◆◆◆

Place the basil and lemongrass into a cocktail shaker and lightly muddle. Add the rest of the ingredients, then add ice cubes and shake enthusiastically until well combined. Double strain into a chilled coupette and garnish with a fresh lemongrass stem.

GARNISH
LEMONGRASS

GLASS
COUPETTE

When Gwladys Gublin created this cocktail, she wanted a comforting drink for autumn: something oaky and orangey, with an acidic touch and a funny story to tell. Le Maudit Français means Bloody French, an expression used in Canada to criticize the French in an affectionate way. This is exactly what's happening in the cocktail: the arrogant and precious French liquor meets the rustic and popular Canadian syrup, and they do a great job together.

Le Maudit Français

30ml (1 ¼ fl oz) 8-year-old Darroze Armagnac

10ml (2 tsp) Don Gonzalo Oloroso sherry

10ml (2 tsp) fresh orange juice

10ml (2 tsp) fresh lemon juice

10ml (2 tsp) maple syrup

1 dash of Bittermens Boston Bittahs

ice

❖❖❖❖◆◆◆◆❖❖❖❖

Place all the ingredients in a cocktail shaker and fill with ice cubes.
Shake well, then double strain into a chilled Champagne flute.
Garnish with a piece of pared orange rind.

GARNISH
ORANGE RIND

GLASS
CHAMPAGNE
FLUTE

This was created by barman Michael Mas, who wanted to make a twist on a Mezcal Manhattan. The addition of the amaro makes this a complex, floral drink, strong and full of smokiness.

Chesterfield

50ml (2fl oz) Mezcal Ki'Mayab
15ml (½fl oz) Amaro Averna
10ml (2 tsp) Carpano Antica Formula
1 dash of Angostura Bitters
ice

••••◆◆◆◆◆◆◆◆••••

Place all the ingredients in a mixing glass and fill with ice cubes. Stir until well chilled and slightly diluted, then strain into a coupette.

GLASS
COUPETTE

The Tête de Mule, originally created by barman Romain Krot, is inspired by the ingredients bartenders would typically use to make a salty cocktail. Tête de Mule, or 'Kind of Stubborn', reflects the taste of this complex cocktail. It's a long drink with layers of salty flavours and hints of spice from the ginger.

Tête de Mule

ice
50ml (2fl oz) Don Fulano Blanco tequila
20ml (¾fl oz) fresh orange juice
20ml (¾fl oz) fresh tomato juice
10ml (2 tsp) agave syrup
ginger beer, to top up

Fill a highball glass with ice cubes, then build the cocktail by adding one ingredient at a time. Stir to chill and dilute slightly, then top up with ginger beer. Garnish with a lime wedge dusted with smoked salt.

GARNISH
LIME WEDGE & SMOKED SALT

GLASS
HIGHBALL

Barman Michael Mas created this twist on a New York Sour by using Guignolet instead of port and sprinkling the drink with powdered liquorice (*Glycyrrhiza glabra*) to add another note to the flavour profile. The result is a slightly complex sour with hints of berry and a touch of liquorice to the finish. The frothy texture makes this a cocktail wonderfully difficult to pronounce but easy to enjoy.

Glycyrrhiza Glabra

1 maraschino cherry
50ml (2fl oz) Rittenhouse Straight Rye 100 Proof whisky
20ml (¾fl oz) fresh lemon juice
15ml (½fl oz) sugar syrup (see page 217)
10ml (2 tsp) egg white
ice
3ml (½ tsp) Guignolet wild cherry liqueur

◦◦◦◦◦◆◆◆◆◆◆◦◦◦◦◦

Crush the cherry in a cocktail shaker, then add the whisky, lemon juice, sugar syrup and egg white. Shake well to combine, then top up with ice cubes and shake again until you have a good frothy texture. Strain into a rocks glass over fresh ice, top with the Guignolet and garnish with liquorice powder.

GARNISH
LIQUORICE POWDER

GLASS
ROCKS

Japon Japon is a journey to Japan in a glass. Nikka Whisky, made in Japan and founded by Masataka Taketsuru, is one of our favourites. In fact, Curio Parlor was the first Nikka Bar outside Japan, and once had over 30 different Nikka whiskies, including some blended specially for us. This cocktail uses the bitterness of the grapefruit and the Campari to bring out the rich, spicy notes of the Nikka from the Barrel.

Japon Japon

40ml (1½fl oz) Nikka Whisky from the Barrel
15ml (½fl oz) fresh pink grapefruit juice
15ml (½fl oz) fresh lemon juice
15ml (½fl oz) sugar syrup (see page 217)
1 dash of grapefruit bitters
ice

Place all the ingredients in a cocktail shaker, fill with with ice cubes and shake enthusiastically. Strain into a rocks glass filled with crushed ice, garnish with 2 lemon leaves and mist the top of the drink with Campari.

GARNISH
LEMON LEAVES & CAMPARI MIST

GLASS
ROCKS

Barman Maxime Potfer created this cocktail to blend two
very different aromas – the creaminess of almond syrup, and the
briny touch of black olives. The result is a sweet and salty journey
as the ice begins to melt and the rocket infuses, creating an intense
herbal aroma. A subtle and elegant cocktail to awaken the senses.

Perpette les Olivettes

1 handful of fresh rocket
40ml (1½fl oz) olive-infused Macchu pisco ⟶
10ml (2 tsp) Dolin dry vermouth
2 dashes of Chuncho bitters
15ml (½fl oz) fresh lime juice
10ml (2 tsp) orgeat syrup (see page 218)
ice

Place 5 drained black
olives in brine in a bottle
of pisco and allow to
infuse for 36 hours.
Remove the olives.

Start by muddling the rocket in a julep tin, then add all the
remaining ingredients, except the ice, to build the cocktail. Add
a large scoop of crushed ice and garnish with a handful of rocket.

GARNISH
ROCKET

GLASS
JULEP TIN

Bartenders Maxime Potfer and Gwladys Gublin created this cocktail for the first Paris Beer Week as a reminder that beer cocktails can be good. The Gueuze Tilquin is tarter than a traditional beer, adding an unexpected layer of flavour. This cocktail starts with a deep wine-like taste and a bitter aroma, then the beer brings in a lightness, floral notes and a hint of sourness.

Le Maillot Jaune

15ml (½fl oz) Buffalo Trace bourbon
30ml (1¼fl oz) Punt E Mes vermouth
30ml (1¼fl oz) Berry Brothers' Quinta de la Rosa tawny port
15ml (½fl oz) fresh lemon juice
2 dashes of Angostura Bitters
ice
Gueuze Tilquin beer, or a similar lambic-style beer, to top up
1 piece of pared orange rind

Place the bourbon, vermouth, port, lemon juice and bitters in a cocktail shaker and fill with ice cubes. Shake vigorously and double strain into a beer snifter. Top with beer and squeeze the orange rind over the drink to release the oils, then discard it.

GLASS
BEER SNIFTER

xperimental Cocktail Club was just the beginning for us. We always wanted another story to tell, another place to call our own. In France, this initially confused people: many thought that the opening of our second bar meant the end of the original ECC. But we had boundless energy and vision and, less than a year later, Curio Parlor was born. At the time, it was uncommon for one operator to have multiple bars in a city. Our aim was to break the mould and continue opening new bars with different concepts, but making sure our bars never felt like a chain.

Tucked away on the Left Bank on the neglected Rue des Bernardins, Curio Parlor was a step in a new direction for us. Cuoco Black returned to Paris to create our interior. Touches of taxidermy graced the walls, and dark, moody seating was tucked beneath exposed beams. Downstairs, a room with a low, arched ceiling housed a small bar where some of the industry's best bartenders mixed drinks for guests seduced by privacy well into the night.

Curio Parlor turned out to be more edgy than ECC, with a very different ambiance. Our basement hosted events and aftershows. We brought in great DJs and enlisted artistic directors Hugues Ferrière and Olivier Coulomb of Buvez Madison to throw parties that kept people talking for weeks. The location was off the beaten track, making Curio Parlor the perfect destination for a party that trailed into the small hours.

We worked behind the bar at Curio, as we did at ECC. During this time, we began to discover Japanese whisky. When we contacted Nikka Whisky to discuss a partnership, we became the first and only Nikka bar outside Japan. Although not all the drinks at Curio Parlor are based on Nikka, there are definite Japanese influences in many of the cocktails, and Japanese whiskies crop up throughout the list. Now closed, Curio holds a special place in our collective hearts and the cocktails produced there are some of our best.

This is Japan meets a Last Word, a nouveau classic cocktail with gin, lime, chartreuse and maraschino. This potent concoction is often enjoyed as the final cocktail of the evening. Here, barman Arthur Combe uses Nikka Pure Malt White to create a balanced cocktail with smoky and vegetal tones, finished with a bit of acidity. Saigo No Kotoba means The Last Word in Japanese.

Saigo No Kotoba

30ml (1¼ fl oz) Nikka Pure Malt White whisky
15ml (½ fl oz) Yellow Chartreuse
15ml (½ fl oz) Luxardo maraschino liqueur
ice

◆◆◆◆◆◆◆◆◆◆◆◆◆◆

Place all the ingredients in a cocktail shaker and fill with ice cubes. Shake until well combined, then double strain into a coupette. Garnish with a piece of pared lime rind.

GARNISH
LIME RIND

GLASS
COUPETTE

The Vieux Rectangle is barman Arthur Combe's signature cocktail. This is his twist on the classic Vieux Carré, with a European interpretation. The result is a fairly sweet concoction on the floral and delicate side, with an anise finish.

Vieux Rectangle

40ml (1½ fl oz) Grosperrin VSOP Cognac
15ml (½ fl oz) Dolin Rouge vermouth
15ml (½ fl oz) Aperol
2 dashes of Angostura Bitters
2 dashes of Peychaud's Bitters
2 dashes of absinthe
ice
1 piece of pared lemon rind

Place all the ingredients in a mixing glass, fill with ice cubes and stir well with a long bar spoon. Strain into a chilled vintage stem glass or mini coupette. Squeeze the pared lemon rind over the cocktail to release the oils, then discard it.

GLASS
VINTAGE STEM

When creating the Sainte Thérèse, barman Arthur Combe was inspired by the French 75, a classic cocktail dating back to Harry's Bar, New York, in 1915. Arthur wished to work with more exotic flavours, so he combined rum with Velvet Falernum and Lillet. The name is simply a nod to the rum used in this recipe.

Sainte Thérèse

30ml (1¼fl oz) Santa Teresa 1796 rum
15ml (½fl oz) Velvet Falernum
20ml (¾fl oz) fresh lime juice
15ml (½fl oz) Lillet Rouge
ice
Champagne, to top up

••••••◆◆◆◆◆◆••••••

Place all the ingredients, except the Champagne, in a cocktail shaker and fill with ice cubes. Shake well, then double strain into a Champagne flute. Top up with Champagne and garnish with pared lime rind.

GARNISH
LIME RIND
GLASS
CHAMPAGNE FLUTE

Pink as Lime is the invention of barman Xavier Lusso.
Using unexpected cult favourite Sanbitter, an Italian sparkling
soda, he created a version of a Cachaça Fizz with a fruity, yet
bitter, taste. The name pays homage to the vivid hot pink colour
of the cocktail, which can be seen from across the room.

Pink as Lime

45ml (1¾fl oz) Engenho da Vertente cachaça
15ml (½fl oz) Velvet Falernum
25ml (1fl oz) fresh lime juice
Sanbitter, to top up
ice

❖❖❖❖◆❖❖❖❖

Place all the ingredients, except the Sanbitter, in a cocktail shaker
and fill with ice cubes. Shake hard until well combined.
Pour over fresh ice into a highball glass, top with Sanbitter and
garnish with pared lime rind.

GARNISH
LIME RIND

GLASS
HIGHBALL

This is a French summer's take on the gin & tonic. 38500 is the postal code of Voiron, the town where Gentiane des Pères Chartreux is made by Carthusian monks. This long drink is bitter and refreshing, offering a great chemistry between the passion fruit and the gentian spirit, balanced by the sweetness of the port nestling in the passion fruit shell.

38500 & Tonic

30ml (1¼fl oz) Beefeater 24 gin

30ml (1¼fl oz) Gentiane des Pères Chartreux

10ml (2 tsp) sugar syrup (see page 217)

1 dash of Angostura Bitters

tonic water, to top up

ice

◆◆◆◆◆◆

Place all the ingredients, except the tonic, in a cocktail shaker and fill with ice cubes. Shake well and strain over fresh ice into a highball glass. Top up with tonic. For the garnish, scoop the seeds out of half a passion fruit and fill the shell with the port.

GARNISH
½ PASSION FRUIT &
NOVAL BLACK PORT
GLASS
HIGHBALL

This is a twist on the Tom & Jerry cocktail. Dating back to the early 1800s, this classic is synonymous with Christmas. In this version, spiced rum replaces brandy, and chocolate milk replaces whole milk. The result is a rum flip, with a nod of schooldays nostalgia from the chocolate milk. A bit naughty for a boozy cocktail, but true cocktail comfort food nonetheless. The name pays homage to *Minus et Cortex*, a 1990s cartoon in the spirit of the *Tom & Jerry* cartoons.

Minus et Cortex

30ml (1¼fl oz) spiced rum

10ml (2 tsp) dark rum

1 egg, beaten

1 dash of Angostura Bitters

10ml (2 tsp) sugar syrup (see page 217)

30ml (1¼fl oz) Cacolac, or other chocolate milk

ice

Place all the ingredients in a cocktail shaker without ice and shake vigorously until well combined. Add some large cubes of ice and shake again. Strain into a coupette and garnish with grated nutmeg.

GARNISH
GRATED NUTMEG

GLASS
COUPETTE

PRESCRIPTION
cocktail ℞ **CLUB**

With momentum pushing us forward, we decided not long after opening Curio Parlor to open our third cocktail bar in Paris. When we first saw what is now Prescription Cocktail Club, we fell in love with it. The place was cool, the location was incredible, set in the midst of Saint Germain des Prés. We stepped into another dimension here – we had two bars, four bar stations, food preparation and a kitchen. There was a lot more to consider but from inception we wanted to keep it artisanal, despite the bar being larger than our first two projects.

Our third opening brought in wunderkind designer Dorothée Meilichzon, who to this day continues to design everything we do. This was one of her first projects and she brought in intimate low seating, fireplaces, patterns and fabrics which are quintessential design elements she still uses with us today. Upstairs, she hid a bar behind a bookcase, dotted small mirror-topped tables next to lush velvety chairs and items plucked from antique markets.

When we opened Prescription we continued to work behind the bar from opening time to closing time, Thursday to Saturday. As time wore on, we slowly relinquished control to a set of seasoned barmen and women, continuing to make each menu a collaborative effort. To this day, while we're not behind the bar creating the cocktails, we take great pride in working with our teams in each city to hear the stories behind each cocktail and taste each new recipe before it makes it onto the menu.

Over time as we began to think of expanding and opening in London and New York, we had to rely on our bartenders to develop cocktail lists and had to trust them to run the bar every night. As scary as it was, we now had the ability to hire bartenders who had been working in other bars, and in other countries, only increasing the amount of amazing ideas we could put in a glass. We also realized that some of our best talent was the men and women

waiting tables and washing glasses, so we began training these people behind the bar, something we continue to do today. Some of those people are now among our best managers around the world. As this happened, our cocktail menus in Paris became more varied and adventurous.

It was around the time that we opened Curio Parlor and Prescription Cocktail Club that we met our fourth business partner, Xavier Padovani. We saw something in him that we all had in us – an unbridled energy and a passion for serving good drinks to everyone. We began hosting parties with him and, in the spirit of our first two bars, we didn't want to stop once the drinks were in the glass, but rather wanted to create an entire experience with music, drinks, people and every amazing detail in between. A few times, we hired a horse and buggy to take people for rides while we served classic recipes from the good old days. It was here that we knew our friendship with Xavier wouldn't just end with the parties we hosted together.

Chet Bacon is inspired by one of our favourite cocktails from New York's PDT (Please Don't Tell), the cocktail bar founded by industry luminary Jim Meehan. It's a cocktail for those who want to reminisce about a proper Southern barbecue, listening to jazz on a long, hot summer's night in Memphis.

Chet Bacon

5ml (1 tsp) maple syrup
5ml (1 tsp) Ilegal mezcal reposado
50ml (2fl oz) bacon-infused Buffalo Trace bourbon (see page 215)
pinch of salt
3 dashes of Angostura Bitters
5 dashes of Memphis Barbecue Bitters
ice

Place all the ingredients in a mixing glass and fill with large cubes of ice. Stir well until a little diluted. Strain into a rocks glass over a single large cube or ball of ice. Garnish with a piece of pared orange rind.

GARNISH
PARED ORANGE RIND

GLASS
ROCKS

This Tiki-inspired cocktail was created by barman Humphrey Bosch, who set out to combine delicate French tastes with French Polynesian Tiki tendencies. He started with the pineapple, ubiquitous in Polynesia, but wanted to add spice and smoke. For the spice, he chose Bittermens 'Elemakule Tiki bitters and a homemade cinnamon, vanilla and star anise syrup which complements the rum. To create a layer of smoky depth, Humphrey used a small amount of mezcal to bring a bit more character to the cocktail.

Smoky Pina

5g (¼oz) fresh pineapple
2–3 sage leaves
20ml (¾ fl oz) fresh lime juice
20ml (¾ fl oz) cinnamon syrup ———→
40ml (1½ fl oz) Appleton's V/X rum
10ml (2 tsp) Ilegal mezcal reposado
4 dashes of Bittermens 'Elemakule Tiki bitters
ice

Place 1 vanilla pod, 3 cinnamon sticks, 2 star anise, the pared rind of 1 orange and 400g (14oz) sugar in a saucepan with 1 litre (1¾ pints) water, bring to the boil, then simmer for 25 minutes. Remove from the heat and allow to cool. Add 60ml (2¼fl oz) Havana Club Especial rum.

Place the pineapple and sage leaves in a cocktail shaker and gently muddle to release the flavours. Add the remaining ingredients, then add ice cubes and shake enthusiastically. Double strain into a rocks glass, add crushed ice and garnish with pineapple leaves.

GARNISH
PINEAPPLE LEAVES

GLASS
ROCKS

This is Tiki on a tropical holiday to Japan. The Nikka is a Japanese single grain whisky with notes of melon and syrup, evened out by vanilla. It plays well with the powerful flavours of coconut, pineapple and sage. The flaming passion fruit garnish is optional: one without a flame is just fine!

The Amazing Tiki

20ml (¾ fl oz) fresh lime juice

⟵ 20ml (¾ fl oz) pineapple & sage syrup

10ml (2 tsp) Suze

40ml (1½ fl oz) Nikka Coffey Grain whisky

2 dashes of coconut bitters ⟶

soda water, to top up

ice

Preheat the oven to 160°C (325°F), Gas Mark 3. Place 1 pineapple, peeled and cut into small chunks, on a baking sheet and sprinkle with 50g (2oz) sugar. Place in the oven for 30 minutes, until golden. Meanwhile, bring 1.5 litres (2½ pints) water to the boil in a saucepan. Add 1.5kg (3lb) sugar and 6 sage leaves. Simmer for 10 minutes, then allow to cool and strain. Add the roasted pineapple and allow it to infuse into the syrup for 30 minutes, then strain.

Place 250ml (8fl oz) Wray & Nephew rum and 250ml (8fl oz) rhum agricole in a large bowl with the flesh from 1 coconut, diced with skin left on, 4 liquorice seeds, 2 caraway seeds and 1 star anise. Allow to infuse for 3 weeks, then strain.

Place all the ingredients, except the soda, in a cocktail shaker and fill with ice cubes. Shake well and strain into a Tiki glass filled with fresh ice cubes, then top up with soda water. For the garnish, place a sugar cube into a passion fruit half, spray with overproof rum and set light to it. Place the flaming passion fruit in the glass with pineapple leaves for colour.

GARNISH
½ PASSION FRUIT,
1 SUGAR CUBE, OVERPROOF
RUM & PINEAPPLE LEAVES

GLASS
TIKI

After Italian barman Cristian Archetti had been experimenting with
liquorice-infused pisco, his fellow barman Romain de Saussure
asked him what he intended to do with it. The resulting drink dances
on the palate. The flavour of the pisco is heightened by the mint and
liquorice earthiness of the Fernet Branca, which in turn is balanced
by the warming maple syrup. Being a julep, the point is to let the ice
melt and dilute the drink, allowing the flavours to mellow and change.
This is a real Italian cocktail.

Picolo's Julep

6 mint leaves
ice
15ml (½fl oz) maple syrup
5ml (1 tsp) Fernet Branca
20ml (¾fl oz) fresh lime juice
50ml (2fl oz) liquorice-infused pisco
(see page 216)

Place the mint leaves in a cocktail shaker and
gently muddle to release the flavour. Add ice
and all the remaining ingredients, shake well and
strain into a julep tin. Add crushed ice and
garnish with a fresh mint sprig.

GARNISH
MINT SPRIG

GLASS
JULEP TIN

Prescription Cocktail Club is in the heart of Saint Germain, a tourist hotbed. Here, we're often asked for something with a little touch of Paris, thus the Fée Fraîche was born. The absinthe, often rough around the edges, is made enjoyable with the addition of mint for freshness, and elderflower cordial and orange bitters for fruitiness. This sour-style drink is rounded out and given a layer of texture with the creaminess of an egg white.

Fée Fraîche

20ml (¾fl oz) Broker's 47 gin
10ml (2 tsp) Nouvelle-Orléans absinthe
10ml (2 tsp) Yellow Chartreuse
5ml (1 tsp) fresh cucumber juice
20ml (¾fl oz) elderflower cordial
6 mint leaves
1 egg white
5 dashes of orange bitters
ice

Place all the ingredients in a cocktail shaker without ice and shake vigorously. Add ice to the shaker and shake again. Double strain into a chilled coupette and garnish with a slice of cucumber.

GARNISH
CUCUMBER SLICE

GLASS
COUPETTE

With three cocktail bars in Paris, we began to realize that our concept needed to morph into something different, or we had to go elsewhere. So we did both. In 2010, we opened our first bar outside Paris, the Experimental Cocktail Club Chinatown in London (see page 78). Two years later, we returned to Paris to open Beef Club & Ballroom, a steakhouse unlike anything else in Paris, with a cocktail bar hidden beneath it.

Ballroom, our cocktail bar hidden in the depths of our first restaurant, is bathed in lush reds, with low ceilings and small rooms for nights spent escaping frenzied evenings and long days at work. Our cocktails here are classic riffs, straightforward and strong, many of which serve up to five people.

Paris has always been our spiritual home, a comforting thought when many of our days are spent in planes and trains, waking up in foreign cities. We've used Paris as the place to try new concepts – cocktail bars, wine bars, restaurants and a hotel. Since the original Experimental Cocktail Club opened in 2007, many of the bartenders who have worked behind the bar there, and behind our other bars, have gone on to open their own bars in Paris or further afield. Our first bartender – Carina Soto Velasquez Tsou – honed her cocktail-making skills at ECC and now has a few bars of her own. Through the years, names like Nicolas de Soto and Joshua Fontaine, now bar owners themselves, refined their drinks repertoire behind our bars, creating some of the best menus Paris and the world has seen. For us, it's the place where we began this journey.

This is part of the Experience series found at the original ECC and a few of our subsequent bars. In this rendition, pisco is the star of this slightly acidic yet fresh and vegetal cocktail. A slight floral flavour and a sweetness is provided by the elderflower. This is a perfect cocktail for any time of the evening.

Experience No. 3

1 lemongrass stem, fat end only
20ml (¾fl oz) fresh lemon juice
20ml (¾fl oz) elderflower cordial
50ml (2fl oz) pisco
2 basil leaves
ice

•••••••◆◆◆◆◆•••••••

Twist the bottom half of a lemongrass stem to extract as much flavour as possible, then put it in a cocktail shaker. Add all the remaining ingredients, top up with ice, then shake vigorously until frost appears on the outside of the shaker. Strain into a chilled coupette and garnish with a fresh basil leaf.

GARNISH
BASIL LEAF

GLASS
COUPETTE

Created by barman Axel Tesch, this is a fresh, fruit-forward dream of a cocktail. The spice-infused Aperol is an unexpected delight, with undertones of cloves, vanilla, anise, nutmeg and cinnamon. The sweet and acidic strawberry punches through the spice, and the Champagne tops off the cocktail with bubbles to awaken the palate. Madame Rêve is a lovely tipple to start the evening.

Madame Rêve

1 large strawberry
20ml (¾fl oz) fresh lemon juice
50ml (2fl oz) spice-infused Aperol ⟶
ice
Champagne, to top up

Place 1 star anise, 1 vanilla pod, 2–3 cloves, 1 whole nutmeg and 1 cinnamon stick in a bottle of Aperol and leave to infuse. The longer you leave it, the stronger the flavour, so test from time to time and strain when you are happy.

•••••◆◆◆◆◆◆•••••

Place the strawberry in a cocktail shaker, muddle, then add the lemon juice and Aperol. Top up with ice, then shake vigorously until frost appears on the outside of the shaker. Double strain into a chilled coupette, top up with Champagne, and serve with a smile.

GLASS
COUPETTE

Père Qui Smashe, created by barman Damien Aries, combines the very traditional French flavour of gentiane with kiwi fruit, mint and absinthe for a fruity, refreshing cocktail. This is perfect for the start of the night to awaken the senses.

Père Qui Smashe

½ kiwi, peeled and chopped
40ml (1½fl oz) Gentiane des Pères Chartreux
20ml (¾fl oz) fresh lemon juice
15ml (½fl oz) sugar syrup (see page 217)
5ml (1 tsp) fresh cucumber juice
4 dashes of Pernod absinthe
ice

Place the kiwi in a cocktail shaker and muddle gently.
Add the remaining ingredients and top up with ice cubes.
Shake well and double strain into a double rocks glass filled
with crushed ice. Garnish with a few mint sprigs.

GARNISH
MINT SPRIGS

GLASS
DOUBLE ROCKS

When barman Romain de Saussure was experimenting with melon syrup, something rather delicate and difficult to use, fellow barman Charlie Brock suggested the addition of Cognac and orgeat to combine with the melon without overpowering its subtle taste. Like many of our cocktails, this drink was the product of an exchange of creativity.

Crusta Charentais

30ml (1¼fl oz) fresh lemon juice, plus extra for the sugar rim
granulated sugar
5ml (1 tsp) orgeat syrup (see page 218)
5ml (1 tsp) Luxardo maraschino liqueur
40ml (1½fl oz) Pierre Ferrand 1840 Cognac
30ml (1¼fl oz) melon syrup
2 dashes of Peychaud's Bitters
ice

Dip the rim of a wine glass in lemon juice to wet it, then in a saucer of sugar to frost the rim. Place the lemon juice and all the remaining ingredients in a cocktail shaker, fill with ice cubes and shake well. Strain into the sugar-rimmed glass and garnish with pared orange rind.

GARNISH
ORANGE RIND

GLASS
WINE GLASS

The Cosmopolitan is a classic that had its heyday at the heels of Carrie Bradshaw. We find it is often ordered by those looking for something sweet and a bit pink. Big Cosmo is Dead is often found on the menu at Ballroom – quadruple the quantities below to serve it as a punch for friends. It's the perfect twist on the pink drink, offering a more bitter tipple but with the same pop of glorious pink.

Big Cosmo is Dead

10ml (2 tsp) falernum ⟶ Place 250g (8oz) sugar and 250ml (8fl oz) water in a saucepan with the pared rind of 10 limes, 8 cloves and 1 star anise. Stir over a medium heat until the sugar dissolves, then bring to the boil. Allow to cool, then add 250ml (8fl oz) white rum and ¼ tsp almond essence and leave to infuse for 24 hours. Strain and store in the refrigerator.

25ml (1fl oz) Aperol
25ml (1fl oz) fresh lime juice
25ml (1fl oz) Fair vodka
2 dashes of cherry bitters
ice

◆◆◆◆◆◆◆◆

Place all the ingredients in a cocktail shaker,
fill with ice cubes and shake until well chilled. Double strain
into a chilled rocks glass. If serving as a punch, make up
a big batch, strain into a bottle and chill in the refrigerator,
or over a large block of ice in a punch bowl
Enjoy soon after making it.

GLASS
ROCKS

This is a Tiki classic done
Ballroom style, a rum-lover's dream
which brings fragrant, fruity and sweet flavours
together in one glass. As with all Mai Tais, it's a boozy
tipple perfect for ending the night on a high note. If you
close your eyes and take a big sip, it may even whisk you away
to the far-off tropics, if only for a moment.

Mai Tai Ballroom

40ml (1½fl oz) rum
20ml (¾fl oz) orgeat syrup (see page 218)
20ml (¾fl oz) fresh lime juice
20ml (¾fl oz) dry Curaçao
2 dashes of Angostura Bitters
5ml (1 tsp) whisky
ice

Place all the ingredients in a cocktail shaker, fill with ice cubes and
shake until frost appears on the outside of the shaker.
Strain into a rocks glass filled with crushed ice and
garnish with a mint sprig, a cherry and
a piece of pared orange rind.

GARNISH
MINT SPRIG,
CHERRY & ORANGE RIND

GLASS
ROCKS

The Concombre Fumant (smoking cucumber) sits somewhere between the classic Tommy's Margarita and a Tequila Sour. The spice kick is balanced by the cool cucumber and creamy egg white, while the mezcal adds a layer of smokiness and makes it difficult to stop at just one. These sour-style cocktails, featuring cucumber, egg white and spice, are often found on the menus at our bars, offering twists on the classic Saint Germain des Prés from ECC Chinatown.

Concombre Fumant

50ml (2fl oz) Don Fulano tequila
25ml (1fl oz) agave syrup
20ml (¾fl oz) fresh lime juice
5ml (1 tsp) fresh cucumber juice
5ml (1 tsp) Green Chartreuse
3 dashes of coriander & chilli-infused mezcal ←
1 egg white
ice

Place 1 bunch of fresh coriander and 2–3 dried chilli peppers in a bottle of mezcal and leave to infuse. The longer you leave it, the stronger and spicier the flavour, so test from time to time and strain when you are happy.

Place all the ingredients in a cocktail shaker without ice and shake vigorously. Then top up with ice and shake again until frost appears on the outside of the shaker. Double strain into a chilled coupette and garnish with a slice of cucumber.

GARNISH
CUCUMBER SLICE

GLASS
COUPETTE

Among the busy streets of London's Chinatown, where the morning air is scented with durian fruit and the evenings bring the aroma of Peking duck, we stumbled on a hidden townhouse which would be the setting for our fourth bar, and our first project outside Paris.

When we had decided to open a cocktail bar in London, we knew we would need someone on the ground to help recreate our Parisian success. Xavier Padovani, a longtime friend and purveyor of a good party, became our fourth partner. At the time, he was spending his days waxing lyrical about the rose and cucumber notes of Hendrick's gin, as he travelled the world as the brand's global ambassador.

The four of us had spent hours walking the streets of London in an attempt to find the perfect place. At one point we had even stood on Gerrard Street and joked that it would be a dream to open the bar right there. When we first stepped foot inside 13a Gerrard Street, we knew in an instant that it was destined to be ours. At the time no one else wanted it, but we immediately saw the potential of this beaten-down venue. We spent months clearing out the rubble, installing bars and adding staircases.

The result was a bar nestled above a Chinese restaurant, with Art Deco touches, vintage Chinese wallpaper, handmade carpets and a hidden piano, a jolly and eclectic mix which fits together like a puzzle, thanks to the keen eye of Dorothée Meilichzon.

ECC Chinatown opened on a cold night in early December 2010. We weren't
sure what to expect. Many people knew what we were doing in Paris, but
London was an unknown territory, already full of amazing bars. The early
days of a new place are always an adventure, and opening a bar in London's
Chinatown meant dealing with Victorian plumbing and questionable
electricity. In the first few weeks, on an evening when the electricity failed,
our DJ Marc Hayward ran home to grab a guitar and played an acoustic
set as he sat on the stairs and everyone sipped cocktails by candlelight.
To this day, it remains one of our most memorable evenings.

Our bar team in London was more international than that in Paris. Whether
it was due to London's more mature bar scene, less of a language barrier or
easier immigration, we now had bartenders hailing from New Zealand,
Australia, South Africa, Portugal, Italy, Canada, Sweden, the UK and of
course France. This collective mindset led to our menus evolving to feature
a wider range of ingredients and techniques.

We made sure that our cocktail menu stepped up to the London game from the start. At the time, the city's cocktail scene was more advanced than that of Paris, so we spent a lot of time creating the first few menus. We quickly realized that in London, people love – really love – to drink, so we needed to start putting out drinks as fast as possible to keep up with the demand. The resulting menus featured some drinks that took a little extra time and effort to make, balanced by a few that could be knocked out quickly.

Our evenings in Chinatown carry on through to the wee hours of the morning and our attention doesn't just stop with the cocktails we make. Most nights of the week, old-school French vibes, classic rock n' roll and songs which wouldn't dare grace the Top 40 drift across our two bars. Each night is a chaotic choreography of drinks expertly crafted a few at a time, Champagne corks popping and a soundtrack to match the perfection of our own little *joyeux bordel* hidden above Chinatown's heaving streets.

This cocktail comes from the second-ever menu at ECC Chinatown and has remained there ever since, quickly becoming an ECC classic. It was originally created by barman Nicolas de Soto during his travels around the world and prior to ECC was known as Nico's Gimlet. It's a refreshing dose of cucumber followed by a fiery kick from the spice tincture. This is a cocktail you could drink all evening, any time of the year.

Saint Germain des Prés

40ml (1½fl oz) Hendrick's gin
20ml (¾fl oz) Saint Germain elderflower liqueur
20ml (¾fl oz) fresh lime juice
20ml (¾fl oz) elderflower cordial
1 egg white
5ml (1 tsp) fresh cucumber juice
1–2 dashes of spice tincture (see page 215)
ice

••••••◆◆◆◆◆•••••

Place all the ingredients in a cocktail shaker without ice and shake vigorously. Then top up with ice and shake again for about 20 seconds. Double strain into a chilled coupette and garnish with a slice of cucumber.

GARNISH
CUCUMBER SLICE

GLASS
COUPETTE

Created by barmen Alex Skarlen and Thor Bergquist, this is inspired by a classic Bourbon Smash but has a Scandinavian twist to celebrate Swedish midsummer and pay homage to Scandi cuisine. This drink works well all year round, but is particularly lovely during summer. Its complex taste features toasted cumin and hints of fresh dill with a slightly salty and acidic finish. This may sound slightly off-putting on the menu, yet as the name suggests, most people come to love it more after every sip.

Stockholm Syndrome

40ml (1½fl oz) Linie aquavit

15ml (½fl oz) cumin & dill-infused Ketel One vodka (see page 216)

20ml (¾fl oz) fresh lemon juice

20ml (¾fl oz) sugar syrup (see page 217)

1 dash of Peychaud's Bitters

pinch of pink Himalayan salt

pinch of black pepper

ice

✦✦✦✦✦✦

Place all the ingredients in a cocktail shaker and fill with ice cubes. Shake vigorously, then double strain into a chilled rocks glass filled with ice. Garnish with a piece of pared lemon rind and a dill stem.

GARNISH
LEMON RIND
& DILL STEM

GLASS
ROCKS

When barman Alex Skarlen was served a Martinez Sour, he began to think about how he could make a more interesting drink by adding ingredients from other classic cocktails. So the Classic Ripoff was born. It is a combination of three classics – the Manhattan (rye and sweet vermouth), the Martinez (gin, sweet vermouth and maraschino) and the Sazerac (rye, Cognac, Angostura Bitters and Peychaud's) – but made into a sour with fresh lemon. It starts with hints of vermouth, moves on to rye, then maraschino, and finishes with some acidity.

Classic Ripoff

40ml (1 ½ fl oz) Pikesville Straight Rye whiskey
20ml (¾ fl oz) Carpano Antica Formula
15ml (½ fl oz) Luxardo maraschino liqueur
20ml (¾ fl oz) fresh lemon juice
5ml (1 tsp) sugar syrup (see page 217)
2 dashes of Angostura Bitters
2 dashes of Peychaud's Bitters
ice

Place all the ingredients in a cocktail shaker, fill with ice cubes and shake enthusiastically. Double strain into a chilled coupette and garnish with a maraschino cherry.

GARNISH
MARASCHINO CHERRY

GLASS
COUPETTE

This is a well-balanced and refreshing fizz with light citrus tones, hints of Amaro and a complex flavour from the tea syrup. It is inspired by the classic Paloma and Gin Fizz, as well as an ECC classic, Winter is Coming (see page 194).

Your Mate

40ml (1 ½ fl oz) Abelha organic cachaça
12.5ml (2 ½ tsp) Amaro Averna
20ml (¾ fl oz) fresh lemon juice
20ml (¾ fl oz) fresh grapefruit juice
2 dashes of orange bitters
20ml (¾ fl oz) lemon verbena & yerba mate tea syrup ⟶
soda water, to top up
ice

Bring 1 litre (1¾ pints) water to the boil in a large saucepan. Remove from the heat, add 1kg (2lb) sugar, 25g (1oz) lemon verbena sprigs and 50g (2oz) yerba mate tea. Stir until the sugar has dissolved, then leave for 1 hour to infuse. Strain and store in the refrigerator.

◦◦◦◦◦◆◆◆◆◦◦◦◦◦

Place all the ingredients, except the soda water, in a cocktail shaker and fill with ice cubes. Shake enthusiastically, then double strain into a chilled highball glass filled with fresh ice cubes. Top up with soda water and garnish with a dried lime wheel.

GARNISH
DRIED LIME WHEEL

GLASS
HIGHBALL

Named after the potion-brewing druid in the Asterix stories,
Getafix might require a few more steps than your typical cocktail.
But once you have the hang of it, it's a refreshing summer cocktail
that can be brought to a friend's house, or served at a summer party
without having to make cocktails all evening. Barman Dan King took
the summery sweet strawberry and combined it with coriander and
celery for a fruit-forward tipple with herbal and vegetal undertones.

Getafix

40ml (1½fl oz) Ketel One vodka

40ml (1½fl oz) Lillet Blanc

Dissolve 5g (⅛ oz) citric acid crystals (available from specialist baking supply stores) in 95ml (3⅓ fl oz) water. ← 30ml (1¼fl oz) 5% citric acid solution

2 dashes of celery bitters

60ml (2¼fl oz) water

30ml (1¼fl oz) strawberry & coriander syrup → Place 500g (1lb) sugar, 500g (1lb) muddled strawberries and 500ml (17fl oz) water in a saucepan and bring to the boil, stirring. Remove from the heat, add 15g (½oz) muddled coriander leaves and leave to infuse for 3–4 hours, or until you achieve the desired flavour. Strain through a fine sieve and store in the refrigerator.

•••••••◆◆◆◆◆◆•••••••

Put a small glass bottle in the freezer. Mix all the
ingredients, except the syrup, in a chilled cocktail
shaker or mixing glass, keeping them as cold as
possible. Take the cold glass bottle from the freezer
and pour in the syrup, then add the remaining
ingredients. Carbonate the cocktail using a
home carbonation system, then seal with a cap.

GLASS
SMALL GLASS
BOTTLE

Handsome Jack, created by barman Chris Tanner, is an elegant, boozy but slightly sweet cocktail. The maple syrup and Chartreuse provide an earthiness, the rye gives it a kick, and the Cognac adds a sweet, smooth finish. It's rather intense but great for cold nights.

Handsome Jack

20ml (¾fl oz) Rittenhouse Straight Rye 100 Proof whiskey
20ml (¾fl oz) Pierre Ferrand Cognac
15ml (½fl oz) Aperol
20ml (¾fl oz) Byrrh
3ml (½ tsp) Green Chartreuse
3ml (½ tsp) maple syrup
2 dashes of Angostura Bitters
2 dashes of Peychaud's bitters
1 piece of pared lemon rind
ice

Place all the ingredients in a mixing glass, fill with ice cubes, and stir gently until slightly diluted. Strain into a chilled coupette and squeeze the lemon rind over the drink to release the oils, then discard it.

GLASS
COUPETTE

95

Winnie the Pooh is a well-balanced, floral version of
a Negroni, so it's quite boozy and bitter. It makes a fine aperitif
all year round. Although inspired by the Negroni, the balance is
different, with light rum and white vermouth rather than the
traditional gin and sweet vermouth. We used to age this drink
for up to a month in a Cognac barrel, but if you don't have a barrel
at home you can still increase the quantities (leaving out the ice) and
age it in a bottle in the refrigerator until ready to serve.

Winnie the Pooh

ice

15ml (½fl oz) Banks 5 Island rum

30ml (1¼fl oz) Campari

30ml (1¼fl oz) Gancia Bianco vermouth

5ml (1 tsp) Fernet Branca

15ml (½fl oz) Cynar

6 dashes of orange bitters (we use a mix of West Indian
Orange Bitters and Regan's Orange Bitters)

Take a rocks glass and add a few cubes of ice. Then add all the remaining
ingredients and stir well to create a lot of dilution. Squeeze a piece of pared
orange rind over the top to release the oils, then place it on top of the ice.

GARNISH
ORANGE RIND

GLASS
ROCKS

To All My Friends

To All My Friends was created at ECC Chinatown as a dedication to friends of the bar. It's a boozier version of a Grasshopper – a complex but light sour with a nice frothy texture. The minty finish is highlighted by small notes of chocolate from the vermouth.

30ml (1¼fl oz) Pierre Ferrand Ambre Cognac
30ml (1¼fl oz) Carpano Antica Formula
15ml (½fl oz) fresh lemon juice
15ml (½fl oz) sugar syrup (see page 217)
5ml (1 tsp) Fernet Branca
1 egg white
ice
soda water, to top up

••••••◆◆◆◆◆•••••

Place all the ingredients, except the soda water, in a cocktail shaker without ice and shake vigorously. Add ice, shake again and double strain into a chilled Champagne flute. Top up with soda and garnish with a mint sprig.

GARNISH
MINT SPRIG

GLASS
CHAMPAGNE
FLUTE

When ECC Chinatown first opened, we decided to create a different menu on Sundays. For us, Sundays are days of long lunches spent with friends rather than late-night parties. The Lavender Ramos, inspired by the Ramos Gin Fizz, is one of the original cocktails on our Sunday menu. It's great for warm, sunny days and is a bit like a dessert, only more refreshing. It's a light, floral fizz with a creamy texture and hints of orange, citrus and of course lavender.

Lavender Ramos

25ml (1fl oz) lavender-infused gin ⟶ Place 2 tsp lavender flowers in a bottle of gin and leave to infuse for 3 hours at room temperature, then strain.
25ml (1fl oz) gin
15ml (½fl oz) fresh lime juice
15ml (½fl oz) fresh lemon juice
20ml (¾fl oz) double cream (heavy cream)
30ml (1¼fl oz) sugar syrup (see page 217)
1 dash orange flower water
1 egg white
ice
soda water, to top up

Place all the ingredients, except the soda water, in a cocktail shaker without ice and shake vigorously. Add ice, shake again for about 30 seconds to get a good creamy texture, then double strain into a chilled pilsner glass. Top up with soda and garnish with a dash of Peychaud's Bitters.

GARNISH
PEYCHAUD'S BITTERS

GLASS
PILSNER

This drink was created by barman Florian Dubois late one night, as the Graveltones played in the background. Jimmy O, one of the band members, wanted something rye-based to sip as he played. Smoke That Rhino combines fruity, smoky and spicy flavours, making it the perfect sour for winter sipping.

Smoke That Rhino

40ml (1½fl oz) Vulson White Rhino Rye

10ml (2 tsp) Rittenhouse Straight Rye 100 Proof whiskey

10ml (2 tsp) ginger syrup (see page 219)

10ml (2 tsp) honey-infused lapsang souchong tea

20ml (¾fl oz) fresh lemon juice

6 dashes of peach bitters

ice

⟶ Place 500ml (17fl oz) honey and 500ml (17fl oz) water in a saucepan and heat to melt the honey. Once combined, add 30g (1¼oz) lapsang souchong tea and leave to infuse for 5–6 minutes. Strain and allow to cool.

◆◆◆◆◆◆◆◆

Place all the ingredients in a cocktail shaker, fill with ice cubes and shake well. Double strain into a double old fashioned glass and add one large cube of ice. Garnish with a piece of pared lemon rind, then spray the top with Laphroaig.

GARNISH

LEMON RIND & LAPHROAIG 10-YEAR-OLD WHISKY SPRAY

GLASS

DOUBLE OLD FASHIONED

Inspired by a classic Bourbon Smash, the Pandan Smash gets an Asian twist from the addition of coriander and pandan leaf. This cocktail is light but savoury and sour, with nutty hints from the pandan-infused Cognac.

Pandan Smash

Place 8 pandan leaves in a bottle of Pierre Ferrand Cognac and allow to infuse for 24 hours, then strain. ← 50ml (2fl oz) pandan-infused Pierre Ferrand Cognac
20ml (¾fl oz) fresh lime juice
20ml (¾fl oz) coconut syrup → Place equal volumes of coconut water and sugar in a saucepan and heat gently, stirring continuously, until the sugar has dissolved. Bring just to the boil, then remove from the heat and leave to cool. Store in the refrigerator.
2 dashes of Angostura Bitters
3 coriander leaves
ice

Place all the ingredients in a cocktail shaker, fill with ice cubes and shake enthusiastically. Double strain into a chilled julep tin filled with crushed ice and garnish with a knot of pandan leaf.

GARNISH
JULEP TIN

GLASS
PANDAN LEAF KNOT

This cocktail is inspired by the Corpse Reviver No. 2, but here you'll get floral notes from the violet alongside the sharp tequila, finished with hints of liquorice.

Nourishment

ice
25ml (1fl oz) Calle 23 Blanco tequila
25ml (1fl oz) Dolin dry vermouth
10ml (2 tsp) fresh lime juice
10ml (2 tsp) fresh lemon juice
25ml (1fl oz) violette mix ⟶ Combine equal volumes of G. Miclo
Violet liqueur, Briottet Crème de
Violette liqueur and sugar syrup
(see page 217) and stir until combined.
Store in the refrigerator.
6 dashes of absinthe

Place all the ingredients in a cocktail shaker,
fill with ice cubes and shake enthusiastically.
Double strain into a chilled coupette.

GLASS
COUPETTE

Rhubarb adds a wonderful layer of complexity to the
Renaissance. Inspired by an Aperol Spritz, this is a refreshing
Champagne cocktail with hints of citrus, rhubarb and salt.
The Renaissance is a lovely drink for spring and summer.

Renaissance

40ml (1½fl oz) Aperol
10ml (2 tsp) Hendrick's gin
20ml (¾fl oz) fresh lemon juice
20ml (¾fl oz) rhubarb syrup (see page 219)
pinch of Himalayan purple salt
ice
Champagne, to top up

Place all the ingredients, except the Champagne,
in a cocktail shaker and fill with ice cubes.
Shake and double strain into a wine glass filled
with fresh ice, top up with Champagne
and add a rhubarb stick to garnish.

GARNISH
RHUBARB STICK

GLASS
WINE GLASS

A simple and delicious twist on the classic Gin Buck,
this drink is served long with plenty of big ice cubes.
The Suze, ginger ale and grapefruit offer a complex
twist for those who might usually order a gin and tonic.

Get Buck In Here

25ml (1fl oz) Hendrick's gin
25ml (1fl oz) Suze
10ml (2 tsp) fresh lemon juice
6 dashes of absinthe
ice
Fever Tree ginger ale, to top up

◆◆◆◆◆◆◆

Place all the ingredients, except the ginger ale, in a cocktail shaker
and fill with ice cubes. Shake and double strain into a highball glass
filled with fresh ice and top up with ginger ale. Garnish with a long
piece of pared grapefruit rind.

GARNISH
GRAPEFRUIT RIND
GLASS
HIGHBALL

From the Depths is inspired by a Trinidad Sour, but is more complex – this drink has warm, dark flavours, with a sweet yet bitter finish. The notes of beetroot, almonds and Angostura Bitters (cinnamon, black pepper and cloves) give this cocktail a wonderfully earthy flavour profile. This is most definitely a cocktail to enjoy during the autumn and winter months.

From the Depths

40ml (1½fl oz) Kraken Black spiced rum
15ml (½fl oz) pressed beetroot juice
15ml (½fl oz) Angostura Bitters
15ml (½fl oz) fresh lime juice
15ml (½fl oz) orgeat syrup (see page 218)
ice

•••••◆◆◆◆◆◆•••••

Place all the ingredients in a cocktail shaker and fill with ice cubes. Shake and double strain into a wine glass filled with fresh ice.

GLASS
WINE GLASS

New York was always a dream for us – it was the inspiration for our first bars in Paris. When we were at university in Montreal in 2005, New York was only a quick hop on a plane away, and we were soon frequenting some of the city's pre-eminent cocktail bars. At the time, New York was on the brink of a cocktail revolution, and as luck would have it, we were there to witness how the industry developed and took shape over the following years.

*A*t the time, places like the Pegu Club, Milk & Honey, and Flatiron Lounge were our escape from the college party norm of tepid beer and bad music. We were amazed by what a proper cocktail could do. It wasn't only the drink, it was the atmosphere, the people, the service, the music, and we knew then that we were hooked. If we had had enough money, we would have opened a bar in New York straight away. But Paris was more attainable for us, so we put New York on hold and returned to France, always promising to go back one day and open our own bar there.

Once we had successful bars in Paris and London, we knew our next step would be New York, no matter how terrifying a jump over the Atlantic might be. After months of trying to find a suitable space we could afford, we landed on a former lounge on Chrystie Street, which happened to be next to The Box. The Box was the venue we used for our first party with Xavier Padovani, for The Fantastic & Ridiculous Monday of the Unusual Rose & Cucumber Society, during his stint as ambassador for Hendrick's gin. In 2012, Experimental Cocktail Club Lower East Side opened its doors.

From day one, we knew we were up against the best – the industry standard – and we had to step up our game to play in the big league. Initially, this meant pushing our boundaries and creating cocktails with five, six, seven ingredients, and complicated tinctures and syrups that took days to make. Now that we're a few years wiser, we've come to realize that it doesn't take a million ingredients to impress New Yorkers. It takes an honest cocktail, great music and good service – exactly what we had originally set out to do.

Instead of hiring local barmen and women, we brought some of our own team with us to New York. This is something most people would never dream of doing, but we have always believed in promoting from within, and we pride ourselves on being able to give our team members the chance to work in multiple countries. Naturally, this gave us the comfort of working with a team we already knew, but it also brought some influences from Paris and London to New York. On the flip side, it also meant we had to go the extra mile to prove ourselves to the locals. No matter how long we have a bar in New York, we will always be up against the guys who were there first and the people who live and breathe the city.

Our interiors in New York, again designed by Dorothée Meilichzon, pay homage to a New York state of mind. Deco touches reminiscent of 1920s Gotham are dotted around the cosy, low-slung seats. There are wallpapers and fabrics in warm golds and greens, marble-topped bars and fireplaces,

and lush velvet and patterned sofas. This flurry of texture, colour and pattern may sound like a jumbled scrapbook of ideas, but the elements all come together to create an oasis away from the bustling Manhattan streets, which are steaming hot in the summer and frozen during the winter months.

Thanks to the layout of the space, we were able to create a private hidden bar tucked behind our cloakroom. We quickly realized that this space, originally designed for private parties and those wishing to escape the noise of a crazy Saturday night, was also the perfect venue to host travelling bartenders keen to showcase their cocktails away from their usual bar. Seating just 13, our secret bar has seen some of the best and brightest in the business, from some of the best bars in the world. Industry leaders such as Shingo Gokan, Ola Carlson, Lynette Marrero, Gary Regan, Jim Meehan and Alastair Burgess, among many others, have shaken and stirred their favourite concoctions on our Between the Sleeves evenings.

New York will always be the foundation on which we built our bars, first in Paris and then in London. It's the birthplace of the drinks that inspired us when we were just 22 years old, spending weekends wandering the streets of Manhattan and dreaming of what the future held for us. At the same time, New York continues to challenge us and is always pushing us to find inspiration in the city where we discovered our dream.

The French Cancan is a creation by Nicolas de Soto that was on our first menu in New York. This cocktail pays homage to his, and our, French roots and is inspired by the dance popular in Paris at the end of the 19th century. This cocktail's red colour is reminiscent of the Moulin Rouge. It is a great early summer cocktail, when rhubarb is ripe and pink.

French Cancan

30ml (1¼fl oz) Fair vodka

30ml (1¼fl oz) Zucca amaro

25ml (1fl oz) rhubarb syrup (see page 219)

25ml (1fl oz) fresh lemon juice

pinch of purple Himalayan salt

ice

Champagne, to top up

❖❖❖◆❖❖❖

Place all the ingredients, except the Champagne, in a cocktail shaker without ice and shake until well combined. Fill a pilsner glass with crushed ice, pour the contents of the cocktail shaker over the ice and swizzle. Top with a dash of Champagne and garnish with a stick of rhubarb.

GARNISH
RHUBARB STICK

GLASS
PILSNER

This is a twist on the Experience No. 1, one of the original cocktails from the Experimental Cocktail Club in Paris. Instead of vodka, we use gin here to give the cocktail an added layer of herbaceous notes. This rendition of the drink appeared on the first few menus we created in New York, as well as on one of the first menus at ECC Chinatown.

Experience No. 2

5 basil leaves
1 lemongrass stem, torn into pieces
60ml (2¼fl oz) Citadelle gin
25ml (1fl oz) fresh lemon juice
25ml (1fl oz) elderflower cordial
ice

Place the basil and lemongrass in a cocktail shaker and lightly muddle. Add the remaining ingredients, then the ice cubes, and shake enthusiastically until well combined. Double strain into a chilled coupette and garnish with a fresh lemongrass stem.

GARNISH
LEMONGRASS

GLASS
COUPETTE

This cocktail, which featured on the opening menu of ECC Lower East Side, was a labour of love. It took time to get right, but it finally came together as a rich concoction of layers – a drink for those who enjoy something a bit on the boozier side.

The Last One

ice
45ml (1¾fl oz) Cardenal Mendoza Spanish brandy
25ml (1fl oz) Bonal gentiane
25ml (1fl oz) Cocchi Barolo Chinato
15ml (½fl oz) Akanone carrot shochu

Fill a rocks glass with big cubes of ice and build this drink one ingredient at a time. Stir to dilute the mixture and garnish with a cherry on a stick.

GARNISH
CHERRY

GLASS
ROCKS

This drink was borne of a discussion between Damien Aries and Edouard Revuz on the merits of a well-balanced cocktail. Many classics are made using equal parts of strongly flavoured ingredients, yet they work really well. Damien and Edouard tried a few different concoctions made using equal parts of something sweet, something bitter, something sour and something strong, and added a bit of cucumber for good measure. The result was the Santa Branca, equal parts surprising and refreshing with tart, floral and minty notes.

Santa Branca

25ml (1fl oz) Fernet Branca
25ml (1fl oz) Plantation 3 Stars rum
25ml (1fl oz) Saint Germain elderflower liqueur
25ml (1fl oz) fresh lemon juice
5ml (1 tsp) fresh cucumber juice
ice

Place all the ingredients in a cocktail shaker, fill with ice cubes and shake well. Strain into a chilled coupette and garnish with a slice of cucumber.

GARNISH
CUCUMBER SLICE

GLASS
COUPETTE

In our Paris cocktail bars, we have created a number of drinks around a main ingredient – the Mazarini cocktails at Prescription, the Experience cocktails at ECC Paris and the Miss series at Ballroom. The Chrystie No.1 was made in New York as the first in a series. This cocktail is fruity, but without too much sweetness. There is a light bitterness and herbal notes from the Aperol and vermouth, and the chipotle adds a smoky taste. The addition of Champagne rounds out the sweetness, creating a lovely balance.

Chrystie No.1

1 ripe strawberry
25ml (1fl oz) Aperol
25ml (1fl oz) shochu
25ml (1fl oz) Cocchi Americano Rosa
25ml (1fl oz) fresh lemon juice
2–3 dashes of chipotle tincture ⟶ Steep 30g (1¼oz) dried chipotle chillies in a bottle of neutral spirit for 4–5 days, then strain with a very fine sieve to remove all the chipotle.
ice
about 25ml (1fl oz) Champagne

Place the strawberry in a cocktail shaker and muddle well. Add the remaining ingredients, except the Champagne, then fill with ice cubes and shake enthusiastically. Double strain into a coupette and top with the Champagne.

GLASS
COUPETTE

The Salt Fashioned was created by Damien Aries, exploring his love for the smoky, peaty Islay whiskies. It's a great choice for neat whisky drinkers, or a way of easing into smoky Islay whisky for those used to something less peaty. This cocktail is made in the same way as a classic Old Fashioned, but the flavours are entirely different. It's certainly quite smoky, but the maple syrup with a touch of sea salt creates a smooth, yet quite dry, taste. The apple bitters give this drink a wonderful dessert-like quality.

Salt Fashioned

60ml (2¼fl oz) Laphroaig whisky
5ml (1 tsp) salted maple syrup → Stir 1 tsp sea salt into 120ml (4fl oz) maple syrup.
3 dashes of apple bitters
ice

Place all the ingredients in a mixing glass, fill with ice cubes and stir with a bar spoon. Strain into a rocks glass with one large cube of ice and garnish with a twist of pared lemon rind.

GARNISH
LEMON RIND

GLASS
ROCKS

This is a refreshing sour-style aperitif, with light bitterness from the gentian and a touch of liquorice and anise flavour from the absinthe.

Salers Smash

ice

60ml (2¼fl oz) Salers gentiane

25ml (1fl oz) fresh lemon juice

20ml (¾fl oz) sugar syrup (see page 217)

4 dashes of absinthe

4–5 mint leaves

Place all the ingredients in a cocktail shaker, fill with ice cubes and shake well. Double strain into a rocks or double old fashioned glass filled with crushed ice and garnish with a fresh mint sprig.

GARNISH
MINT SPRIG

GLASS
ROCKS OR DOUBLE
OLD FASHIONED

This flip-style cocktail is the perfect wintertime drink.
The whole egg creates a wonderfully creamy texture and
the combination of bourbon, port, almond and coffee make
this the ideal cocktail for sipping next to a log fire.

Midnight Snack

1 egg

15ml (½fl oz) orgeat syrup (see page 218)

15ml (½fl oz) Bittermens coffee liqueur

15ml (½fl oz) tawny port

45ml (3 tbsp) bourbon

ice

❖◆❖◆❖◆❖◆❖

Place all the ingredients, except the ice, in a cocktail shaker
and shake vigorously. Top up with ice, then shake hard for
10–15 seconds. Double strain into a chilled coupette and grate
a large piece of butter cookie on top.

GARNISH
GRATED BUTTER
COOKIE

GLASS
COUPETTE

Here barman Damien Aries and his team set out to achieve the same balance found in a Last Word cocktail. This classic drink mixes ingredients which individually have a very strong flavour profile, but which combine to create a fresh and crisp result.

Arrackiri

30ml (1¼fl oz) Batavia arrack
30ml (1¼fl oz) fresh lime juice
15ml (½fl oz) agave syrup
15ml (½fl oz) Yellow Chartreuse
15ml (½fl oz) mezcal
5 dashes spice tincture (see page 215)
ice

◆◆◆◆◆◆◆◆◆◆

Place all the ingredients in a cocktail shaker and fill with ice cubes. Shake until well chilled, then double strain into a chilled coupette. Garnish with a slice of cucumber.

GARNISH
CUCUMBER SLICE
GLASS
COUPETTE

When we first set foot on the White Isle, it was an island undergoing transformation. What was once a hippie hideout had become an all-night party, full of DJs from around the world, but it slowly seemed to be returning to its roots. We were intrigued.

*B*ack in Paris, a lot of the people who came to our bars were spending weekends in Ibiza. It was no longer just about the club scene; people were raving about little hidden restaurants and beaches that rivalled the Caribbean. What was evident was the lack of a decent cocktail: the drinks being poured into glasses in these hidden gems and on those glorious beaches didn't seem to live up to the beauty of the island.

Experimental Beach is our version of Experimental Cocktail Club gone on holiday. In our eyes, Ibiza was overdue for a proper cocktail served up on the beach. We spent long hours during cold winters dreaming up a concept for a summer destination where we could bring our *joyeux bordel* and mix it with beachy island life. After years of escaping to Ibiza to recover from harsh winters, we opened our bar in Salinas National Park on a windswept day in April 2013.

Awash with light blue and white décor, Experimental Beach Ibiza has a hippie chic ambiance, with sand under your feet. Sunbeds are scattered along the shore and a marooned boat festooned with golden fairy lights serves as the bar, giving off the kind of warm, hazy glow you only

find at a beach bar. The view of the sunset here is one of the best on the island, as the sun sinks below the horizon and guests sip on cocktails well into the night.

Our cocktails in Ibiza are made to the same high standards as those in Paris, London and New York: we use the best spirits and we make our own fresh juices every day. But that's about as similar to our other menus as we get here. In Ibiza, we can be less serious, so our drinks are more playful. Our cocktails here, like the décor, are the summer counterparts to the drinks found in our dark, cosy bars. Our seaside guests demand something more fun or perhaps something sweeter, leaving the Manhattans and Negronis for city drinking. Our Ibiza menu reflects a lighthearted take on a few classic cocktails.

In Ibiza, people travel with an entourage. Unlike the smaller groups of two or four guests we are used to in London, New York and Paris, in Ibiza we serve up cocktails to groups of 10, all lounging on sunbeds. And because it's more fun to share one big cocktail, many of the drinks on our menu can be

scaled up for a crowd. Traditional punch bowls are replaced with frozen pineapples and custom-designed conch shells.

The vibe in Ibiza, like the décor and the cocktails, is a step away from the usual atmosphere in our bars. The music played in the beachside DJ booth is a chilled-out, summer-holiday selection of our signature mix of hard-to-find tunes. Many of the DJs from our other bars travel to Ibiza to play a few sets during the summer, pumping out lighter notes of jazz, bossanova and old school vibes – music that goes with drinking cocktails at sunset.

The guests who frequent our summer paradise are often regulars in London, Paris and New York. On the White Isle, they step off the plane looking for an escape, whether it's in the all-night clubs or in the hippie, hedonistic hangouts on the island. Without fail, sooner or later they come for a sunset session at Experimental Beach, where they can stretch out on sunbeds and enjoy the beachside twists on our signature cocktails.

The Aperol Spritz is one of the most popular cocktails for a European summer day: a juicy red-orange goblet that can be seen from a distance. Barman Inko Garat added coconut water and vanilla for a fresh, beachy twist on the original. This version looks very much like the original, but the taste offers a deeper complexity with a summery attitude.

Spritz Me Up

ice
40ml (1½fl oz) vanilla-infused Aperol ⟶
20ml (¾fl oz) Noilly Prat Dry
20ml (¾fl oz) fresh lime juice
20ml (¾fl oz) fresh grapefruit juice
60ml (2¼fl oz) coconut water
Cava, to top up

Split 1 vanilla pod in half lengthways to reveal the seeds, then place it in a bottle of Aperol. Leave to infuse for a week before use and leave the vanilla pod in the bottle.

◆◆◆◆◆◆◆

Place some ice cubes in a wine glass and add all the remaining ingredients, except the Cava, to build the cocktail. Stir gently, top up with Cava and garnish with a piece of dried coconut.

GARNISH
DRIED COCONUT

GLASS
WINE GLASS

This cocktail originated at the Prescription Cocktail Club in 2011, and originally included Green Chartreuse and agave syrup spiced with cayenne. When Pasteque Asteque was added to the menu at Experimental Beach, barman Inko Garat replaced the Chartreuse with a local liqueur called Hierbas, and added a coriander and cayenne spice tincture.

Pasteque Asteque

40ml (1½fl oz) Ocho tequila
2 dashes of cayenne & coriander spice tincture ⟶ Wearing gloves, slice open 200g (7oz) fresh cayenne peppers or other long red chillies and infuse them with a bottle of mezcal and a bunch of fresh coriander for up to 72 hours. Strain the liquid through a fine sieve.
5ml (1 tsp) Hierbas
40ml (1½fl oz) fresh watermelon juice
20ml (¾fl oz) fresh lemon juice
15ml (½fl oz) agave syrup
ice

Place all the ingredients in a cocktail shaker and fill with ice cubes. Shake until well combined, then strain into a rocks glass over fresh ice. Garnish with a sprig of rosemary.

GARNISH
ROSEMARY SPRIG

GLASS
ROCKS

When we opened Experimental Beach, we wanted to pay homage to one of the world's oldest cocktails. The forerunner of Spain's famous sangria, Sangaree dates back to the 18th century. Barman Inko Garat set out to create a twist on the Sangaree with elements of the Caipirinha, so this recipe uses passion fruit and cachaça, both native to Brazil. It also includes a Caribbean liqueur and dry vermouth from France, used in place of the wine.

Brazilian Prescription

40ml (1½fl oz) Cachaça Yaguara

15ml (½fl oz) Noilly Prat Dry

2.5ml (½ tsp) Pimento Dram allspice liqueur

20ml (¾fl oz) honey

20ml (¾fl oz) fresh lemon juice

ice

•••••••◆◆◆◆•••••••

Place all the ingredients, except the ice, in a julep tin and stir to combine. Add a lot of crushed ice and garnish with half a passion fruit.

GARNISH
PASSION FRUIT

GLASS
JULEP TIN

The Strawberry Daiquiri is the quintessential drink to enjoy on a hot summer's day by the sea. When we opened Experimental Beach, we decided to put this classic cult favourite, reserved only for holiday drinking, on the menu. For us, the most important thing was to make sure it was made in the freshest way possible, using homemade ingredients and fresh juices. The result is a daiquiri suitable for sipping until the sun goes down, and in some cases, after.

Strawberry Daiquiri

50ml (2fl oz) Havana 3 Stars rum
1 strawberry
40ml (1½fl oz) grenadine syrup (see page 218)
20ml (¾fl oz) fresh lime juice
ice

Place the rum, strawberry, grenadine and lime in a blender and blend until well combined. Pour over crushed ice in a large wine glass and garnish with a strawberry on a cocktail umbrella.

GARNISH
STRAWBERRY

GLASS
WINE GLASS

The Pineapple Express made its first appearance on the Experimental Beach menu in May 2013, for the opening of the beach bar and restaurants. This cocktail is served in a frozen pineapple, with a few straws to share. This is a simple twist on the classic Piña Colada, a beach staple, but is a bit less sweet and a little bit stronger.

Pineapple Express

1 pineapple
80ml (3fl oz) Appleton V/X rum
20ml (¾fl oz) Kraken Black spiced rum
60ml (2¼fl oz) fresh pineapple juice
20ml (¾fl oz) fresh lemon juice
large spoonful of coconut ice cream
40ml (1½fl oz) passion fruit syrup
ice

Place 1 litre (1¾ pints) passion fruit pulp and seeds in a saucepan with 100g (3½oz) sugar and heat to 70°C (158°F), stirring, until a syrup forms. Strain through a fine sieve and leave to cool. Store in the refrigerator.

Cut the top off the pineapple and scoop out the flesh, which can be used to make pineapple juice. Place the hollowed-out pineapple in the freezer and leave until frozen. Place all the remaining ingredients, except the ice, in a blender and blend until well combined. Put a scoop of crushed ice into the pineapple and pour the blended ingredients over the ice.

GARNISH
A FEW STRAWS

GLASS
FROZEN PINEAPPLE

When we embarked on this journey in 2006, we wanted to work with old friends to create our version of the *joyeux bordel* – a unique mix of late nights, great music and amazing cocktails. When we first opened our bars, we spent our evenings serving drinks and at closing time, we went home to an apartment we shared. Friendship is the reason we're here today, and it goes without saying that the new friendships we've forged along the way mean the world to us.

When we opened the original Experimental Cocktail Club on Rue Saint-Sauveur, the first people to sit at the bar as we tirelessly made cocktails were some of our best friends. With thirsty appetites and honest feedback, they were our first set of guinea pigs, offering us their unwavering support often late into the night.

Now with bars in Paris, London, New York and Ibiza, our lives are a far cry from the days we shared a small apartment on Rue Saint-Martin in the 3rd arrondissement. Now we can't always be in the same place at once, as with time came growing families and different cities. However, we're lucky enough to be able to travel, whether researching a new project, finding hidden gems in new cities or checking in on our own cocktail bars.

Over time spent in our favourite bars around the world, we've met other bar owners, bartenders, journalists and people who simply love a good cocktail. When we arrive in a new city, often under the heavy weight of jetlag, a familiar face and a stiff drink make for a warm welcome. It's essential for our sanity to have friends everywhere – someone to share a meal with or

a drink late at night; someone to catch up with, whether it's been a month or five years since we last met. For us, there truly is nothing worse than arriving somewhere, half enjoying a dinner for one and contemplating a night out with no one to reminisce about the last time you saw each other.

When we set out to write this book, we immediately thought that some of the friends we met along the way, who gave us advice during tough times, or raised a congratulatory glass on an opening night, should have a say in these pages. This chapter isn't about the cocktails on our menus, but the cocktails made or enjoyed by our friends around the world.

Gin Basil Smash
Joerg Meyer, Hamburg

Created a few years back by the legendary Joerg Meyer, this cocktail is one that we can't help ordering when we touch down in Mr Meyer's fair city. It's an honest cocktail with a healthy dose of gin, evened out by sugar and lemon and taken up a notch with a large handful of basil. This is a cocktail to take you through the night, helped by the fact that there's something green in it – so it can't be bad, right?

handful of basil
60ml (2¼fl oz) gin
30ml (1¼fl oz) fresh lemon juice
20ml (¾fl oz) 2:1 sugar syrup (see page 217)
ice

Place the basil in a cocktail shaker and muddle gently. Add the remaining ingredients, then the ice cubes and shake well. Double strain over fresh ice in a rocks glass and garnish with a basil leaf.

GARNISH
BASIL LEAF

GLASS
ROCKS

The St Nicholas Manhattan was created by Julien Gualdoni, better known as Papa Jules, who runs the bar at the famed Cliff restaurant on the island of Barbados. This cocktail is a Bajan twist on a Manhattan and is perfect for anyone who dreams of boozy beachside cocktails. The cocktail is best enjoyed in the balmy Barbados heat.

St Nicholas Manhattan

Papa Jules, Barbados

470ml (16fl oz) St Nicholas Abbey 12-year-old rum
235ml (8fl oz) Cinzano Rosso
470ml (16fl oz) coconut water
6 dashes of Angostura Bitters

◆◆◆◆◆◆◆

Mix all the ingredients together, stir well and store in the freezer.
Once well chilled, pour straight into a chilled coupette and garnish
with a twist of pared orange rind. This recipe is enough for 5–6 servings.

GARNISH
ORANGE RIND

GLASS
COUPETTE

Michael Mas worked with us at Experimental Cocktail Club and has become more than just a barman to the group. Now a long-time friend, he's moved on from our bars but his Inna Di Yard is one of our favourite cocktails. He created this drink after a trip to St Petersburg. He and a Russian friend and barman wanted to make a Trinidad Sour but realized that Angostura is too expensive in Russia. As a result, they opted to use Salers and created a new recipe.

Inna Di Yard
Michael Mas, Paris

30ml (1¼fl oz) Salers gentiane
15ml (½fl oz) Wray & Nephew rum
2 dashes of orange bitters
30ml (1¼fl oz) orgeat syrup (see page 218)
30ml (1¼fl oz) fresh lime juice
ice

Place all the ingredients in a cocktail shaker and fill with ice cubes. Shake vigorously, then pour over fresh ice in a rocks glass. Garnish with a nice, large twist of pared lime rind.

GARNISH
LIME RIND

GLASS
ROCKS

Jim Meehan, the legend behind PDT, is a long-time friend and advocate of our bars. He's since moved on to the greener pastures of Portland but we still try to visit PDT when we're in New York. Although Jim is no longer behind the bar, we can still order up one of our favourites, the Mezcal Mule, from his successor Jeff Bell. A backyard barbecue in a glass, this spicy passion fruit and cucumber buck gets its smoky quality from mezcal distilled from agaves roasted in underground ovens heated by wood-fired stoves.

Mezcal Mule
Jim Meehan, Portland

20ml (¾fl oz) fresh lime juice

3 cucumber slices

ice

45ml (1¾fl oz) Del Maguey Vida mezcal

30ml (1¼fl oz) ginger beer (see page 219)

20ml (¾fl oz) Boiron passion fruit purée

15ml (½fl oz) agave syrup

•••••◆◆◆◆◆◆•••••

Place the lime juice and cucumber slices in a cocktail shaker and muddle. Add the remaining ingredients and ice cubes and shake well. Strain into a rocks glass filled with ice and garnish with a piece of candied ginger and a slice of cucumber on a stick. Finish with a pinch of chilli powder.

GARNISH
CUCUMBER SLICE, CANDIED
GINGER & CHILLI POWDER

GLASS
ROCKS

Carina Soto Velasquez Tsou was one of the first people,
other than us, working behind our bars, and we put a huge amount
of faith and trust in her expertise. Carina has now gone on to
open her own places in Paris, and she and her team have put their
mark on the city's nightlife. When we're not in our own bar, we often
check in at hers – not only for a familiar face, but a good drink.

Blind Date at Chelsea
Carina Soto Velasquez Tsou, Paris

1 strawberry

1 raspberry

40ml (1½fl oz) Grosperrin VSOP Cognac

15ml (½fl oz) Hayman's sloe gin

10ml (2 tsp) Luxardo maraschino liqueur

20ml (¾fl oz) fresh lemon juice

10ml (2 tsp) sugar syrup (see page 217)

ice

Place the strawberry and raspberry in a cocktail shaker and muddle gently.
Add all the remaining ingredients, fill with ice cubes and shake well. Double
strain into a chilled coupette and garnish with a piece of pared lemon rind.

GARNISH
LEMON RIND

GLASS
COUPETTE

Down a set of grungy stairs in the heart of East London sits a small, unassuming bar owned and operated by Alastair Burgess. Since opening, Happiness Forgets has become a go-to bar for many people in the drinks industry, and its laid-back attitude complements a menu of well-made drinks. The Perfect Storm is one of Alastair's signature cocktails and is a straightforward, spicy concoction that packs a punch.

Perfect Storm
Alastair Burgess, London

50ml (2fl oz) dark rum
5ml (1 tsp) La Vieille Prune, or La Vieille Mirabelle
20ml (¾fl oz) fresh lemon juice
15ml (½fl oz) honey syrup (see page 217)
15ml (½fl oz) ginger juice ⟶ Use an electric juicer to extract the juice from a piece of fresh root ginger, measure the volume and add an equal volume of caster sugar. Stir to dissolve.
ice

••••◆◆◆◆◆◆••••

Place all the ingredients in a cocktail shaker, fill with ice cubes and shake well. Strain into a highball glass with fresh ice cubes and garnish with a wedge of lemon.

GARNISH
LEMON WEDGE

GLASS
HIGHBALL

When we make it to the Left Coast, which isn't often, Shaun is a familiar face and he pours a great drink. The Meat Hook packs a punch and was inspired by the new classic Red Hook. The name reflects the neighbourhood around Shaun's bar at L'Abattoir, in the past the site of the city's main butchery and meat-packing district.

Meat Hook

Shaun Layton, Vancouver

45ml (1¾fl oz) Rittenhouse Straight Rye 100 Proof whisky

25ml (1fl oz) Punt E Mes vermouth

5ml (1 tsp) maraschino liqueur

10ml (2 tsp) Ardbeg 10-year-old whisky

ice

◆◆◆◆◆◆◆◆◆◆

Place all the ingredients in a mixing glass, fill with ice cubes and stir until well chilled and slightly diluted. Strain into a chilled coupette and garnish with a cherry.

GARNISH
CHERRY

GLASS
COUPETTE

High above the streets in Tokyo's Ginza district is a tiny bar, only big enough for a few guests lucky enough to snag a seat. Behind the bar stands Mr Ueno. Despite the small size of the bar, the cocktails he creates are so expertly put together that he now has a global following. Although we don't often get to Tokyo, when we do, Bar High Five is one not to miss. His Huntsman cocktail is a straightforward mix of bourbon, Chambord and orange bitters – a perfect pick-me-up to battle the jetlag beast.

Huntsman

Hidetsugu Ueno, Tokyo

45ml (1¾fl oz) 101 proof bourbon whiskey

15ml (½fl oz) Chambord

few dashes of orange bitters

ice

❖❖❖◆◆❖❖❖

Place all the ingredients in a mixing glass, fill with large ice cubes and stir until well chilled and slightly diluted.

Strain into a chilled coupette.

GLASS
COUPETTE

Nico is an old friend who worked with us in Paris, London and New York before opening his own bar. When he wasn't behind our bars, he was travelling the world finding inspiration for new cocktails. This is one of Nico's complex creations, made with ingredients that seem like they don't belong in a glass. He got the idea of mixing cocoa and mushroom when he tried a dark chocolate infused with shiitake. The name pays homage to Takeshi, a bartender at ECC New York, who moved back to Japan.

Take Is Going Back to Japan
Nicolas de Soto, New York

2.5ml (½ tsp) Pedro Ximenez El Maestro sherry
60ml (2¼fl oz) shiitake-infused Great King Street whisky
5ml (1 tsp) cocoa-infused maple syrup
2 dashes of black walnut bitters
ice

Place 600ml (1 pint) maple syrup, 200ml (7fl oz) water and 100g (3½oz) cocoa nibs in a saucepan and bring to the boil. Simmer for 5 minutes, then leave to cool overnight. Strain.

Add 5 dry shiitake mushrooms to a bottle of whisky, allow to infuse for 3 days, then strain.

•••••◆◆◆◆◆•••••

Pour the sherry into a rocks glass and swirl it around without any ice, effectively 'rinsing' the glass with the sherry. Once the glass is well rinsed, pour the leftover liquid out. Place all the remaining ingredients in a mixing glass and fill with ice. Mix well with a spoon, then strain into the rinsed rocks glass and add one large cube of ice. Garnish with a cherry or two on a stick.

GARNISH
CHERRIES
GLASS
ROCKS

A trip to the Pacific Northwest wouldn't be complete without stopping off at Canon, a bar stocked to the ceiling with some of the best spirits, bitters, whiskies and liqueurs. At the helm is our good friend Jamie Boudreau, and his Washington's Mule is a long, refreshing drink perfect for quenching your thirst after a long flight, or even just a long day. The spicy ginger beer brings out the flavours of the apple brandy, and each sip brings you closer to a crisp autumn day in Seattle.

Washington's Mule
Jamie Boudreau, Seattle

45ml (1¾fl oz) Laird's apple brandy, or calvados
15ml (½fl oz) fresh lime juice
3 dashes of Angostura Bitters
Cock 'n Bull ginger beer, to top up
ice

Place all the ingredients, except the ginger beer, in a cocktail shaker and fill with ice cubes. Shake until well chilled, then strain into a Collins glass with fresh ice. Top up with ginger beer and garnish with a bright green lime wedge.

GARNISH
LIME WEDGE

GLASS
COLLINS

Classics

It's rare for a cocktail to spring to life out of thin air, something totally new and never consumed before. You will find a flip, a fizz, a sour or a swizzle at the heart of most of our drinks, and probably every other drink on a cocktail menu around the world. It's not that there aren't any new ideas, but when it comes to mixing a cocktail, some things simply work.

*T*he men and women behind our bars grew up with a passion for food and drink, and as a result they have an innate curiosity for developing something new to put in a glass, relishing that split-second look of pleasure on the face of the drinker at the first sip of a cocktail. Hailing from all over the world, our bartenders are influenced by their own cultures and those that surrounded them. They are on a constant search for fresh ideas, and often look to their travels, their friends or a spirit they've stumbled upon for inspiration.

Bartenders are some of the best-travelled people in the world. They function on little sleep and can chat up nearly anyone. Upon arriving in a new place, they are on a mission to find something that excites them, something undiscovered. New flavours and ideas emerge when a bartender returns to the bar fresh from a trip to some far-flung place, having spent time in a bustling city or on a hidden beach.

Our cocktail menus go through a slight change every six to eight weeks, allowing our bar staff to be continuously creative. Amid the tinctures, infusions and new ideas from around the world, the classics begin to shine through each menu.

When you pick up one of our menus, it might at first appear to be a daunting list of unfamiliar spirits, syrups and tinctures. On closer inspection, however, you will realize that most of our cocktails start from a classic style, and our bartenders have created a twist on something simple and straightforward.

This chapter offers a peek inside the eccentric minds of our bartenders. It's a look at how we get from A to B: sometimes it's a simple case of replacing one ingredient with another, but sometimes we combine two classics to create a brand new cocktail. Recipes for classic cocktails may differ between bars, or from book to book. These recipes will create drinks made to the spec to which we would make them at our bars.

For many, the Negroni is the quintessential go-to drink – simple and straightforward, but boozy and bitter. The Tonka Fievre, which often features on the ECC Chinatown menu, is a twist on this classic. The substitution of tequila and mezcal for gin and the addition of coffee beans and Fernet Branca amp it up with earthy, smoky and herbal flavours.

Negroni

ice
30ml (1¼fl oz) Beefeater gin
25ml (1fl oz) Campari
20ml (¾fl oz) Carpano Antica Formula

Fill a rocks glass with ice, then add the remaining ingredients.
Stir until slightly diluted and garnish with pared lemon and orange rind.

GARNISH LEMON & ORANGE RIND   GLASS ROCKS

Tonka Fievre

5ml (1 tsp) tonka-infused Del Maguey Vida mezcal
30ml (1¼fl oz) Calle 23 Blanco tequila
20ml (¾fl oz) Carpano Antica Formula
20ml (¾fl oz) Campari
2.5ml (½ tsp) Fernet Branca
a few coffee beans
ice

Grate 1 tonka bean into a bottle of mezcal and leave to infuse for 8 hours, then strain through a very fine sieve.

Place all the ingredients in a mixing glass, fill with ice cubes and stir.
Strain into a rocks glass filled with ice and garnish
with pared lemon rind.

GARNISH LEMON RIND   GLASS ROCKS

The Super East Side is a twist on the classic East Side cocktail. In the Super, the elderflower liqueur and cordial replace the sugar, giving it a more dry taste, while the spice tincture adds complexity. Our version is blended and served over crushed ice, rather than shaken, to complement the long, hot days in Ibiza.

East Side

4 cucumber slices
3–6 mint leaves
50ml (2fl oz) gin
25ml (1fl oz) fresh lime juice
20ml (¾fl oz) sugar syrup (see page 217)
ice

Place the cucumber in a cocktail shaker and muddle, then add the remaining ingredients and fill with ice. Shake and double strain into a chilled coupette. Garnish with a fresh slice of cucumber.

GARNISH CUCUMBER SLICE   GLASS COUPETTE

•••••◆◆◆◆◆•••••

Super East Side

40ml (1½fl oz) Citadelle gin
20ml (¾fl oz) Saint Germain elderflower liqueur
2 dashes of spice tincture (see page 215)
3 cucumber slices
1 mint leaf
20ml (¾fl oz) elderflower cordial
20ml (¾fl oz) lime juice
ice

Place all the ingredients, except the ice, in a blender and blend until well combined and a bit frothy. Place some crushed ice in a large wine glass and pour the mixture over the ice. Garnish with a slice of cucumber.

GARNISH CUCUMBER SLICE   GLASS WINE GLASS

Requiem for a Drink was inspired by a Harvard, a Manhattan made with Cognac. In our version, the marsala and dark chocolate add more complexity and give the cocktail a richer flavour profile. This drink is a perfect partner for a cold winter's night.

Harvard

50ml (2fl oz) Pierre Ferrand Ambre Cognac
20ml (¾fl oz) Carpano Antica Formula
2 dashes of Angostura Bitters
ice

Place all the ingredients in a mixing glass, fill with ice cubes and stir until well chilled and slightly diluted. Strain into a chilled coupette and garnish with a cherry.

GARNISH CHERRY   GLASS COUPETTE

Requiem for a Drink

ice
50ml (2fl oz) Pierre Ferrand Ambre Cognac
10ml (2 tsp) Cynar
10ml (2 tsp) marsala
5ml (1 tsp) Mozart Dark Chocolate liqueur
5ml (1 tsp) St Elizabeth Allspice Dram

Place all the ingredients in a mixing glass, fill with ice cubes and stir until well chilled and slightly diluted. Strain into a chilled rocks glass and garnish with a star anise.

GARNISH STAR ANISE   GLASS ROCKS

La Medicación is inspired by the classic Penicillin, with a nod to the classic Tommy's Margarita as made by the famed Julio Bermejo. The result takes the agave influences of the Tommy's and pairs it with the ginger spice found in the Penicillin. Here we use mezcal, a smoky, agave-based spirit that references both the tequila-based Tommy's Margarita and the smoky Scotch-based Penicillin.

Penicillin

50ml (2fl oz) Scotch whisky
10ml (2 tsp) honey syrup (see page 217)
10ml (2 tsp) ginger syrup (see page 219)
20ml (¾fl oz) fresh lemon juice
ice

••••◆◆◆◆◆◆••••

Place all the ingredients in a cocktail shaker and fill with ice cubes. Shake and double strain into a rocks glass filled with fresh ice. Garnish with a piece of candied ginger and mist the top of the drink with Laphroaig or another smoky whisky.

GARNISH
CANDIED GINGER &
LAPHROAIG MIST

GLASS
ROCKS

Tommy's Margarita

50ml (2fl oz) tequila
20ml (¾fl oz) fresh lime juice
10ml (2 tsp) agave syrup or 20ml (¾fl oz) agave water
(see page 216)
ice

Place all the ingredients in a cocktail shaker and fill with ice cubes. Shake and double strain into a rocks glass filled with fresh ice, then garnish with a lime wedge.

GARNISH
LIME WEDGE

GLASS
ROCKS

La Medicación

45ml (1¾fl oz) Calle 23 Reposado tequila
10ml (2 tsp) Ramazzotti amaro
3 dashes of St Elizabeth Allspice Dram
10ml (2 tsp) agave water (see page 216)
10ml (2 tsp) ginger syrup (see page 219)
15ml (½fl oz) fresh lime juice
ice

Place all the ingredients in a cocktail shaker and fill with ice cubes. Shake and double strain into a rocks glass filled with fresh ice and mist the top of the drink with 5 sprays of Del Maguey Vida mezcal.

GARNISH
DEL MAGUEY VIDA
MEZCAL MIST

GLASS
ROCKS

The Pondicherry Mule moves away from Moscow and over to India with a cardamom infusion. A thirst quencher at aperitif time – or at any time in the evening – this fresh and slightly spicy cocktail has travelled with us from Paris to Ibiza to New York.

Moscow Mule

50ml (2fl oz) vodka
20ml (¾fl oz) fresh lime juice
15ml (½fl oz) ginger syrup (see page 219)
5ml (1 tsp) sugar syrup (see page 217)
ice
ginger beer, to top up

Place all the ingredients, except the ginger beer, in a cocktail shaker and fill with ice cubes. Shake and double strain into a highball glass filled with fresh ice. Top with ginger beer, and garnish with a lime wedge and 1 dash of Angostura Bitters.

GARNISH LIME WEDGE & ANGOSTURA BITTERS   GLASS HIGHBALL

Pondicherry Mule

15ml (½fl oz) caster sugar
20ml (¾fl oz) fresh lime juice
5ml (1 tsp) ginger cordial
50ml (2fl oz) cardamom-infused Fair vodka ⟶ Place about 3g (1tsp) green cardamom seeds in 1 bottle of vodka and leave to infuse for 5 hours, then strain.
3 dashes of Angostura Bitters
ice
ginger beer, to top up

Place all the ingredients, except the ginger beer, in a cocktail shaker and fill with ice cubes. Shake until well combined, then strain over fresh ice in a highball glass. Top up with ginger beer and garnish with star anise.

GARNISH STAR ANISE   GLASS HIGHBALL

Winter is Coming is a tribute to *Game of Thrones*, a favourite among the team at ECC Chinatown. This drink was inspired by the Paloma, but the tequila is replaced by aquavit and Amaro Montenegro is added, giving it a Scandi-Italian twist. The original Paloma is made with Ting, a Jamaican grapefruit drink, but we use grapefruit juice and soda water instead.

Paloma

20ml (¾fl oz) fresh lime juice, plus extra for the salt rim
salt
50ml (2fl oz) tequila
20ml (¾fl oz) fresh pink grapefruit juice
20ml (¾fl oz) agave water (see page 216)
ice
soda water, to top up

Dip the rim of a highball glass in lime juice to wet it, then in a saucer of salt to frost the rim. Place the lime juice and all the remaining ingredients, except the soda water, in a cocktail shaker, fill with ice cubes and shake well. Strain into the highball glass over fresh ice and top up with soda water. Garnish with a lime wedge.

GARNISH LIME WEDGE   GLASS HIGHBALL

Winter is Coming

40ml (1½fl oz) Linie aquavit
20ml (¾fl oz) Amaro Montenegro
20ml (¾fl oz) fresh lemon juice
20ml (¾fl oz) fresh grapefruit juice
20ml (¾fl oz) sugar syrup (see page 217)
ice
soda water, to top up

Place all the ingredients, except the soda water, in a cocktail shaker, fill with ice cubes and shake well. Double strain into a chilled highball glass over fresh ice cubes and top up with soda water. Mist the top of the drink with 4 sprays of violette liqueur.

GARNISH VIOLETTE LIQUEUR MIST   GLASS HIGHBALL

Smoke & Mirrors is inspired by the Blood & Sand, but with a Mexican influence: it's made with mezcal instead of Scotch. This cocktail has a lovely smoky flavour that marries well with the bitter spiciness of the grapefruit.

Blood & Sand

25ml (1fl oz) Scotch whisky
25ml (1fl oz) Cocchi Vermouth di Torino
25ml (1fl oz) Cherry Heering liqueur
25ml (1fl oz) fresh orange juice
ice

Place all the ingredients in a cocktail shaker, fill with ice cubes and shake well. Double strain into a chilled vintage stem glass or coupette and squeeze a twist of pared orange rind over the drink to release the oils, then use to garnish.

GARNISH
ORANGE RIND
GLASS
VINTAGE STEM

Smoke & Mirrors

25ml (1fl oz) Del Maguey Crema de Mezcal
25ml (1fl oz) Cherry Heering liqueur
25ml (1fl oz) Punt E Mes vermouth
25ml (1fl oz) fresh grapefruit juice
1 piece of pared orange rind
ice

Place all the ingredients in a cocktail shaker, fill with ice cubes and shake well. Double strain into a chilled coupette and squeeze a piece of pared orange rind over the top to release its oils, then discard.

GLASS
COUPETTE

Vintage Cocktails

Tucked away behind our bars in London and New York are bottles of spirits made before any of us were born. Some spirits might change slightly as the angel's share evaporates but most taste largely as they did back when they were bottled and sealed. A drink made with these vintage spirits is a unique opportunity to taste what a cocktail would have been like well before most of us were old enough to sit at a bar – a cocktail time machine.

*T*hese days many distilleries rely on technology to ensure each bottle tastes exactly like the last. While the rise of cocktail culture throughout the world has made mechanization and computerized quality control necessary, some spirits are still distilled by hand, and these are often found behind our bars. But it's getting harder and harder to find handcrafted spirits made in the same way they were fifty or sixty years ago.

Our foray into the world of vintage spirits began in 2010 during a trip to Lyon to visit our dear friend Georges Dos Santos, better known as Jojo, and his partner at the time Paul Delorme, of Antic Wine. This is where we first sipped Noilly Red Vermouth from the Fifties and Sixties. A larger-than-life character, Jojo offered us some of his most interesting bottles to taste. When he realized that these vintage spirits were more than just personal interest for us, he and Paul began sourcing some bottles for our back bar in London.

At first, sitting on our bar, these bottles offered just a visual journey back in time. We would offer little sips here and there, often to other bartenders or regulars. As time passed, we put a few drinks on the menu. When we opened Experimental Cocktail Club in New York, we decided to source some vintage spirits in America, and once again put a few vintage cocktails on the list.

Today, the vintage spirits we have behind our bars range from Chartreuse Tarragone, a rare Chartreuse which was produced in Tarragona, Spain, after the Carthusian monks were expelled from France, to Eau d'Arquebuse, a medicinal white herbal spirit. Over time, we've struck gold with vintage Clacquesin, a dark pine liqueur with a peaty taste, and have served Cointreau, Noilly Red and Gordon's from the late 1950s, and Grosperrin from the 1800s.

The recipes in this chapter are simply a glimpse at a few of our favourite classics. As much as we would love you to raid your granddad's secret stash, it's essential to ensure that vintage spirits are still in good condition and have not spoiled over time. This is often the case with lower-alcohol spirits. When we find vintage spirits, we go through a painstaking process to understand where they came from and how they were stored before we serve them in our bars in London and New York.

As the name suggests, this is a beautiful gem of a cocktail. Probably dating back to the late 1800s, this cocktail appears in Harry Johnson's 1882 *Bartenders' Manual*. The original calls for equal measures of each ingredient but our version here puts a slight twist on this classic.

Bijou

45ml (1¾fl oz) 1950's Gordon's gin
20ml (¾fl oz) 1960s Cinzano Antica Formula
5ml (1 tsp) 1970s Green Chartreuse
2 dashes of Angostura Bitters
ice

Place all the ingredients in a mixing glass, fill with ice cubes and stir until well chilled and slightly diluted. Strain into a chilled vintage stem glass or coupette and garnish with a twist of pared lemon rind.

GARNISH
LEMON RIND

GLASS
VINTAGE STEM
OR COUPETTE

This is a cocktail with an obscure past – no bartender or bar is credited with this potent minty creation. Some believe it was invented in the Prohibition era, with the mint added to hide the smell of alcohol, but the drink appears in Tom Bullock's 1917 *Ideal Bartender*, long before everyone was drinking behind closed doors.

It is usually made with white crème de menthe, but at ECC Chinatown we have a beautiful old bottle of the green stuff dating back to the 1950s, so our Stinger can be seen from across the room.

Stinger

40ml (1½fl oz) 1950s Martell XO Cognac

15ml (½fl oz) 1958 Amer Picon

15ml (½fl oz) 1950s crème de menthe

ice

••••••◆◆◆◆◆•••••

Place all the ingredients in a cocktail shaker and fill with ice cubes.
Shake well and strain into a chilled vintage stem glass or coupette.
Garnish with a mint leaf, for an extra burst of green.

GARNISH
MINT LEAF

GLASS
VINTAGE STEM

Around 1850, Sewell T. Taylor owned a bar in New Orleans called the Merchants Exchange Coffee House. He decided to leave his business and start importing spirits instead, one of which was Sazerac-de-Forge et Fils. A chap called Aaron Bird took over the bar and changed its name to Sazerac House. The house speciality – the Sazerac – was a riff on the original 'Cock-Tail' (or liquor, sugar, bitters and water) using Taylor's Sazerac and bitters made by local chemist Antoine Peychaud.

Sazerac

2.5ml (½ tsp) absinthe
30ml (1¼fl oz) 1950s Martell XO Cognac
30ml (1¼fl oz)
1963 Canadian Club Rye
5ml (1 tsp) demerara syrup
3 dashes of Peychaud's Bitters
ice
1 piece of pared lemon rind

Place 2 volumes, for example 2 cupfuls, of demerara sugar and 1 volume (1 cupful) of water in a saucepan and heat until the sugar dissolves. Remove from the heat, allow to cool and store in the refrigerator.

Pour the absinthe into a rocks glass and swirl it around without any ice, effectively 'rinsing' the glass with the absinthe. Once the glass is well rinsed, pour the leftover liquid out. Place all the remaining ingredients in a mixing glass, fill with ice cubes and stir until slightly cold and not too diluted. Strain into the rinsed rocks glass and squeeze the lemon rind over the drink to release the oils, then discard it.

GLASS
ROCKS

The story goes that Ted Kilgore, then at the Monarch Restaurant in Maplewood, Missouri, made this drink for a co-worker who asked him for something to help the pain of his rough night disappear. Ted handed him a Purgatory with a warning: 'If you drink very many of these in succession, you will experience this drink's namesake. You have been forewarned.' According to *Difford's Guide Cocktails*, it was adapted from a recipe written by Gary Regan in his column in the *San Francisco Chronicle*.

Purgatory

50ml (2fl oz) 1963 Canadian Club rye whiskey

10ml (2 tsp) 1950s Bénédictine DOM

10ml (2 tsp) 1970s Green Chartreuse

ice

❖❖❖◆◆◆◆◆❖❖❖

Place all the ingredients in a cocktail shaker and fill with ice cubes. Shake well and strain into a chilled coupette. Squeeze a twist of pared lemon rind over the top of the drink to release its oils, then use to garnish.

GARNISH
PARED LEMON RIND
GLASS
COUPETTE

This modern-day classic was made by Milk & Honey's Sam Ross in New York. This stunning cocktail, although created not long ago, takes a walk back in time using vintage spirits at ECC Lower East Side. It's a robust concoction and one to savour, taking time over each sip.

Chet Baker

60ml (2¼fl oz) 1940s Leeds & Wakefield rum

5ml (1 tsp) 1960s Cinzano Antica Formula

5ml (1 tsp) honey syrup (see page 217)

2 dashes of orange bitters

ice

••••••◆◆◆◆◆•••••

Place all the ingredients in a mixing glass, fill with ice cubes and stir until well chilled. Strain over ice in an old fashioned glass and garnish with a twist of pared lemon rind.

GARNISH
LEMON RIND

GLASS
OLD FASHIONED

Basics

TECHNIQUES & INGREDIENTS

Citrus rind is often used to garnish a drink, as it adds aroma as well as looking decorative. Always use unwaxed fruit, as wax will prevent the release of oils when squeezing the rind or making a twist.

Double straining is used to remove ice shards from a drink to prevent over-dilution, or to remove pieces of fruit or other ingredients. After it has been made, the drink is poured out through the strainer of the cocktail shaker, through a fine sieve and into the glass.

Frosting Some of our cocktails are served in glasses with frosted rims. The frosting can be either salt or sugar, depending on the drink. To stick the salt or sugar to the rim of the glass, wet the rim using lemon or lime juice or another ingredient from the drink. Then dip the rim of the glass in a saucer of sugar or salt and shake off the excess.

Ice is used in a cocktail shaker or mixing glass to cool the ingredients rapidly while the drink is being mixed. Always use large ice cubes, as the larger the cubes, the less dilution of the drink. Crushed ice can be used in a serving glass to pour the cocktail over, but never use it in a shaker.

Misting We mist some of our cocktails before serving as a kind of garnish to add aroma to the drink. When a drink is misted with Laphroaig or mezcal, for example, it adds a smoky nose without the taste. Place the liquid in a small pump-action diffuser and simply spray on top of the cocktail just before serving.

Muddling is a technique used to release flavour and fragrance from fruit, herbs and spices. It is usually done with a muddler, although the handle of a wooden spoon can also be used. A muddler is rather like a long, flat-ended pestle made from wood, metal or plastic.

TINCTURES, INFUSIONS & SYRUPS

We strive to always use the freshest ingredients we can, so homemade tinctures, infusions and syrups are a must in many of our cocktails. Perfecting these recipes means we can get just the right flavour profile, giving our drinks more depth as well as a personal touch. In some cases, it's possible to substitute products bought off the shelf, but it's easier to control the sweetness, bitterness or acidity of something we create ourselves.

Spice Tincture

200g (7oz) red bird's eye chillies
1 bottle of Wray & Nephew rum

Slice the chillies open, then infuse in the bottle of rum for up to 72 hours. Strain to remove the chillies and seeds.

Bacon-infused Bourbon

10 rashers of smoked bacon
1 bottle of Buffalo Trace bourbon

Grill the bacon until crisp, then add the bacon and the fat from the pan to the bottle of bourbon. Allow to infuse for 5 hours, then place in the freezer until the fat is hard. Pour into a large sieve lined with three layers of filter paper or kitchen paper and allow to drip through slowly. This may take up to 48 hours.

Liquorice-infused Pisco

5 liquorice sticks
1 bottle of pisco

Place the liquorice sticks in a cocktail shaker and muddle gently to bruise them.
Place them in the bottle of pisco and allow to infuse for 48 hours, then strain.

Cumin & Dill-infused Vodka

2 tsp cumin seeds
1 bottle of Ketel One vodka
large handful of fresh dill

Place the cumin seeds in a dry frying pan and heat, stirring continuously, until lightly browned.
Place in the bottle of vodka with the dill and leave to infuse for 24 hours. Strain.

Agave Water

**Agave syrup is a great sweetener that can be used as a sugar substitute.
The taste goes particularly well with tequila and mescal.**

2 parts agave syrup
1 part water

Place 2 volumes, for example 2 tablespoons, of agave syrup and 1 volume (1 tablespoon)
of water in a small bowl or jug and stir until the syrup dissolves.

Sugar Syrup

1 part sugar
1 part water

Place 1 volume, for example a cupful, of sugar and 1 volume of water in a saucepan over a medium heat and stir until the sugar dissolves. Remove from the heat, allow to cool and store in a bottle in the refrigerator.

2:1 Sugar Syrup

2 parts sugar
1 part water

Place 2 volumes, for example 2 cupfuls, of sugar and 1 volume (1 cupful) of water in a saucepan over a medium heat and stir until the sugar dissolves. Remove from the heat, allow to cool and store in a bottle in the refrigerator.

Honey Syrup

100ml (3½fl oz) honey
50ml (2fl oz) water

Place the honey and water in a small saucepan and heat gently, just until the honey dissolves in the water. Allow to cool.

Grenadine Syrup

1 litre (1¾ pints) fresh pomegranate juice
1kg (2 lb) sugar
50g (2oz) strawberries
1 tsp rosewater
50ml (2fl oz) pomegranate molasses
pared rind of 1 lemon
pared rind of 1 lime
pared rind of 1 orange

Place the pomegranate juice in a blender with the sugar, strawberries, rosewater, pomegranate molasses and the pared rinds. Blend until smooth, then transfer to a saucepan and heat to 90°C (200°F). Maintain at that temperature for 1 hour, then cool. Store in the refrigerator.

Orgeat Syrup

Almond syrup is available commercially but this homemade version is particularly good.

500g (1lb) blanched almonds, lightly toasted
750ml (1¼ pints) water
caster sugar
30ml (2 tbsp) brandy
5ml (1tsp) almond essence
2 drops of orange blossom water

Place the almonds and water in a large bowl and leave to soak for 6 hours. Transfer the mixture to a blender or a food processor and blend until smooth. Pass the mixture through a fine sieve, pressing the almonds to extract all the water. Measure the volume of liquid, add an equal volume of sugar, heat and allow to dissolve. Add the brandy, almond essence and orange blossom water. Allow to cool, and store in the refrigerator for up to 1 week.

Rhubarb Syrup

1kg (2lb) sugar
1kg (2lb) rhubarb, sliced
750ml (1¼ pints) water

Place the sugar, sliced rhubarb and water in a saucepan and bring to the boil.
Reduce the heat and simmer until the rhubarb is soft. Strain and press to
extract the juice from the rhubarb, then allow to cool.

Ginger Syrup

75g (3oz) demerara sugar
50ml (2fl oz) water
150ml (6fl oz) fresh root ginger juice

Place the sugar and water in a small saucepan and bring to the boil, stirring to dissolve the sugar.
Once the mixture has boiled, remove from the heat and allow the syrup to cool. Meanwhile, wash
and juice the ginger root, leaving the skin on. Mix the juice with the cooled syrup.

Ginger Beer

700ml (1 pint 2fl oz) boiling water
240ml (7½fl oz) peeled and grated fresh root ginger
3 tbsp light brown sugar
20ml (¾fl oz) fresh lime juice

Place the water, ginger and sugar in a bowl, cover and leave to infuse for 1½ hours.
Pass the mixture through a chinois or very fine sieve, squeezing the pulp until it is
nearly dry to extract as much of the liquid as possible. Add the lime juice, then pour
into a clean bottle and store in the refrigerator.

INDEX

INDEX

To every person who has taken part in this happy mess, be it making the drinks or drinking them, this book is for you.

••••◆◆◆◆◆◆◆••••

An Hachette UK Company
www.hachette.co.uk
First published in Great Britain in 2015
by Mitchell Beazley, a division of
Octopus Publishing Group Ltd
Carmelite House
50 Victoria Embankment
London EC4Y 0DZ
www.octopusbooks.co.uk
www.octopusbooksusa.com

Distributed in the US by
Hachette Book Group
1290 Avenue of the Americas
4th and 5th Floors
New York, NY 10020

Distributed in Canada by
Canadian Manda Group
664 Annette St
Toronto, Ontario,
Canada M6S 2C8

ISBN 978 1 84533 968 5

A CIP catalogue record for this book is available from the British Library

Printed and bound in China

10 9 8 7 6 5 4 3 2 1

Publishing Director Stephanie Jackson
Art Director Yasia Williams-Leedham
Designer Steve Leard
Senior Editor Alex Stetter
Special Photography Addie Chinn
Writer & Prop Stylist Julie Padovani
Illustrator Grace Helmer
Senior Production Manager Peter Hunt

The publisher would like to thank the following companies
for the use of their wallpapers in this book:
Original design by ARTE wallcoverings, shown on
pages 110, 120, 126–27, 137, 188–89, 212–13
Cole & Son, Flamingos 66/6045, shown on pages
89, 180–81 (www.cole-and-son.com)
Osborne & Little, shown on pages 48–49, 64–65, 78, 198–99
Nina Campbell distributed by Osborne & Little shown
on pages 27, 37, 62-63 (www.osborneandlittle.com)

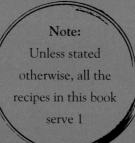

Note:
Unless stated
otherwise, all the
recipes in this book
serve 1